Not by Bread Alone

Daily Reflections for Lent 2009

Kath

LITURGICAL PRESS

Collegeville, Minnesota

www.litpress.org

Nihil Obstat: Rev. Robert C. Harren, J.C.L.
Imprimatur: ✠ Most Rev. John F. Kinney, J.C.D., D.D., Bishop of St. Cloud, Minnesota, May 20, 2008.

Cover design by Ann Blattner.

ISSN: 1550-803X

ISBN: 978-0-8146-3180-5

Introduction

Christ's life easters in us throughout the year, but it tends to get obscured. Losing sight of the understanding and wisdom that are his Spirit's gifts in us, our minds are often dark. Sidetracked by seemingly irresistible desires for immediate satisfaction or comfort, our wills weaken and keep us from doing the good his Spirit inspires. Lent is a special time of purification and enlightenment not only for catechumens preparing for baptism but for all of us who will renew our commitment to our baptismal life in Christ at Easter. Baptismal life unites us with Christ in the loving dance of the Trinity: Father, loving to the utmost, ecstatically pouring out Self in an eternal living Breath of Love to the Son, who blissfully returns that Sigh of Infinite Love. This is Easter life, our inheritance as God's children—ours for the receiving, nothing we have to earn. The human vocation is to live this life of love every moment, freely receiving and freely giving the Love dwelling within us. "Getting the hang of this" in all the particulars of daily life—whether eating and drinking, working or resting, rejoicing or suffering, traveling or staying at home, raising a family or living alone or in a community, through gain and loss, sickness and health, birth and death—is sometimes exhilarating and rewarding, sometimes exhausting and painful. Failure to get in sync with this dance of Love is a necessary part of the process.

Learning life is like learning a language, the language of Love: it is not ours to invent, but ours to integrate into consciousness and expression with the help of our teacher, the Holy Spirit. Lent is a time to give ourselves over more intentionally to the Holy Spirit's instruction. The two traditional Christian ways of learning this language are asceticism and prayer. Asceticism, from the Greek *askesis*, means exercise. It refers to the spiritual exercises that open us to God's life within, exercises that with God's grace will free us from the compulsions or obsessions that keep Love from filling our consciousness and expressing itself in all our actions. Our efforts at prayer, whether in words or in an interior silent attraction of our will to God, are part of our asceticism, as are fasting and almsgiving.

To fast, pray, and give alms are the three practices Christ invites us to during Lent. They help us get in sync with the dance of Love, learn the language of Love, open ourselves more fully to the Easter spring of joyful Love that is always bubbling up within and around us even when it is overgrown by weeds. Grace to give ourselves to these practices is given through Scripture and sacrament, and in all the daily interchanges of our lives. As we try to be faithful to some ascetic practice we will surely sometimes fail. When we do, it is important not to let discouragement make us give up. Our failures in the process of learning are part of that "happy fault," extolled in the Easter *Exsultet*, that "necessary sin of Adam, which gained for us so great a Redeemer." From our experience and from the light of Scripture and Christian tradition, we know that Divine Mercy and Love will triumph. Easter victory comes through Jesus' failure in death. Christ identifies with us at our weakest so that God's merciful Love may prevail in us.

Setting out together on this Lenten journey, the journey of life, we will learn to let God be God, to want only the triumph of divine Love in our selves, our Christian communities, and world.

> This we can do in a fitting manner by refusing to indulge evil habits and by devoting ourselves to prayer with tears, to reading, to compunction of heart and self denial. During these days, therefore, we will add to the usual measure of our service something by way of private prayer and abstinence from food or drink, so that each of us will have something above the assigned measure to offer God of his [her] own will *with the joy of the Holy Spirit* (1 Thess 1:6). In other words, let each one deny himself [herself] some food, drink, sleep, needless talking and idle jesting, and look forward to holy Easter with joy and spiritual longing. (RB 49:4-6).

Starting Over

Readings: Joel 2:12-18; 2 Cor 5:20–6:2; Matt 6:1-6, 16-18

Scripture:
Even now, says the LORD,
   return to me with your whole heart,
      with fasting, and weeping, and mourning. (Joel 2:12)

Reflection: Much of life is "starting over"! On Ash Wednesday we are especially aware of that. Our monastery shares a campus with quite a large college student population. The church here is usually packed for the Ash Wednesday Eucharist and distribution of ashes—more so than for any Sunday celebration during the year. This phenomenon may be the result of many motivations. High on the list, I suspect, is the desire in many of us to "start over." We want to be and to do better than we have been. We really want to return to God (see Joel 2:12), to be more faithful to the Gospel call to love as Christ loves. God knows that this desire resounds in each of our hearts. United in the love of Christ we are, in fact, a community filled with desire to live in the divine goodness in spite of the fact that we get distracted and out of touch with that deep desire.

No matter where we are or what we are doing, today we hear the urgency of Joel's trumpet blast and the proclamation of this annual fast (Joel 2:15). It is a compelling invitation to turn our personal and ecclesial attention "now," on "the day of salvation" (2 Cor 6:2), to the deeper life that is within us, our baptismal life in the loving dance of the Trinity. That means once again renewing our efforts to loosen our hearts' grip on the things that separate us from the love of God and our sisters and brothers, our compulsive and excessive individual and social pursuits of the good things of this world—food, drink, fame, and fortune. It means taking up Jesus' invitation in today's gospel to pray, fast, and give alms, doing so unobtrusively, willingly, joyfully, "in secret" with God who lives, as the poet Jessica Powers says, "in the secret of [our] soul[s]."

Divine goodness and love will touch our world through our successful efforts—and, yes, even in our failures, as we keep our hearts fixed in God who is "gracious and merciful," "slow to anger," and "rich in kindness" (Joel 2:13).

Meditation: Take some time out today to consider how you would like to start over.

Prayer: Gracious and merciful God, our beginning and our end, you live within us and our world. During this season of Lent and Easter grant us the grace to let go those things that separate us from you and each other, so that as your people we may manifest your secret, loving presence in our world. Amen.

Too Much Kills

Readings: Deut 30:15-20; Luke 9:22-25

Scripture:
Then [Jesus] said to all,
   "If anyone wishes to come after me, he must deny
      himself
   and take up his cross daily and follow me.
For whoever wishes to save his life will lose it,
   but whoever loses his life for my sake will save it."
      (Luke 9:23-24)

Reflection: Every day there is set before us the choice between "life and prosperity, death and doom" (Deut 30:15). Sometimes what looks like life is death, and what may at first look and feel like doom is real prosperity at a true and deep level! Unlike the assessment of Mae West, who is supposed to have said, "Too much of a good thing is—wonderful," our experience proves the opposite! Too many chocolate bars make the eater sick. Still, we may sometimes think that one can never have too much money, too much property.

Most of the world's resources are controlled by 10 percent or less of the world's population, for the most part those living in rich nations. The "too much" of the 10 percent is causing misery and death among many of the rest. And the stress, competition, and need for more and more controlling power, including military force and violence on the part of the few, deprives even them of real life and happiness. Back in 1948 in the "U.S. Policy Planning, Study #23," George Kennan, a leading United States policy planner, articulated a policy that seems to have gained momentum. He said:

> [W]e have about 50% of the world's wealth, but only 6.3% of its population. . . . In this situation, we cannot fail to be the object of envy and resentment. Our real task in the coming period is to devise a pattern of relationships which will permit us to maintain this position of disparity.

Today's gospel calls us to repent, that is, to turn around, to look at the world from another, more inclusive viewpoint: "to save our lives by losing them." That call invites us to choose real life and joy by turning away from prosperity gained at the expense of others. This call is addressed to us as individuals, and also to all of us as church and nations. Jesus challenges us to this in the gospel today because he loves us and wants to love with the infinite, inclusive love of God through his Spirit within us.

Meditation: Reflect on areas of "too much" in your personal life. Think about some ways you could help change the world's imbalance of resources. Entrust all this to God and ask for light and courage to do what you can to change.

Prayer: Giver of all good gifts, enlighten our minds and hearts through the power of your Spirit so that we may know how and have the desire to share the world's goods equitably. This we pray through Christ in the Holy Spirit. Amen.

Love Is Effusive

Readings: Isa 58:1-9a; Matt 9:14-15

Scripture:
This, rather, is the fasting that I wish:
   releasing those bound unjustly . . .
Setting free the oppressed . . .
Sharing your bread with the hungry . . .
   and not turning your back on your own. (Isa 58:6-8)

Reflection: God is Love. Love's nature is to be effusive, generous, kind, caring, self-giving, and always fully open to and welcoming of the other. The inner life of God as Trinity is a life of total generous giving and total welcoming receptivity in Love. That is the life we share through creation in God's image, and through baptism into that divine reality. We are living in God, in Love; and God, Love, is living in us. But God will not force us to accept that Love. We are free. If in our daily lives we refuse not only to live generously but even choose to live unjustly with our sisters and brothers, we are cutting ourselves off from God, from Love, and from true happiness—not because God wants it, but because we, in our mistaken notions of what will make us happy, choose to do so.

   Often we cry out that God does not hear our prayer. God hears us, but we cannot hear the divine response, the "Here

I am," "right with you," because we are out of earshot. It is as if we have closed the ports and the borders of our country to generous and mutual self-giving and receiving, and taken up residence in a walled and barricaded country of our own "national interests." God is always speaking, but we have shut God out of our homeland and chosen to spend our share of inheritance the way we would like, on our own narrow interests without regard to what anyone else needs. It may be that our injustice is a wall that muffles the divine voice.

Today we are invited to break down those walls not only by fasting from food but also by dismantling our personal and communal self-serving pursuits and attitudes that are blind to the needs of others. When we take action to help our sisters and brothers secure their just share of the earth's resources, we will be opening our ears to hear that divine voice of compassion saying "Here I am!" (Isa 58:9).

Meditation: Take some time to settle down, quietly observe your breathing. As your inhaling and exhaling slow down, repeat trustingly, "God of love and compassion, open my heart to receive and give your love!"

Prayer: Searcher of minds and hearts, you know us better than we know ourselves. Show us the ways we shut our ears to your voice, our hearts to your love. Through the power of your Spirit within us, open our inner ears to your, "Here I am," and open our eyes to your presence in our sisters and brothers. We pray in union with one another in Christ. Amen.

February 28: Saturday after Ash Wednesday

Repentance Heals

Readings: Isa 58:9b-14; Luke 5:27-32

Scripture:
Jesus said to them in reply,
 "Those who are healthy do not need a physician, but the
  sick do.
I have not come to call the righteous to repentance but
  sinners." (Luke 5:31-32)

Reflection: In the face of Scripture's relentless call in these first days of Lent to look head-on at our unjust and oppressive attitudes and behavior as individuals, human communities, and nations, these words of Jesus to the Pharisees and their scribes are comforting. He is saying, "I know you are sinners. I do not find it at all distasteful to be with you; in fact I want to come to your house! It is for you I have come. You can be healed through my inspiration and help. I am, after all, the Great Physician."

Whether we are sinners like the tax collectors who deliberately extort from others more than they owe or can give— whether in money, service, or emotional response—or whether we are sinners like the Pharisees whose religious practice is impeccable but who miss the deeper call to act justly, Jesus wants to heal all. Our healing can come only through our positive response to his call to repentance.

The word used here for repentance, as in other places in the New Testament, is *metanoia*. It comes from two Greek words, *meta*, "beyond," and *nous*, "mind." In order to be open to the deep healing power of the Spirit of God who lives in us in Christ, we have, in a sense, to be "out of our minds!" We are invited to let go our usual mindset, go beyond our ordinary ways of thinking about and seeing reality. The Pharisee mind in us ordinarily thinks "I can do it! I can secure my place, my status, through perfect religious practice." The tax-collector worldview in us is certain it can achieve the good life by taking any means necessary to shore itself up with material, emotional, or intellectual resources. We are being invited to drop those mindsets, go beyond them, accept our inability to make ourselves secure, and to place all our trust in God, praying with the psalmist "Hear me, LORD, and answer me, / for I am poor and oppressed. / . . . [S]ave your servant who trusts in you" (Ps 86:1, 2b).

Meditation: Set aside twenty minutes today for silence and solitude. As you settle down, be aware of your thoughts and feelings as they arise. Calmly accept each and let them go by turning your desire to trust in God as you repeat interiorly, "Save your servant who trusts in you."

Prayer: Christ Jesus, you are our great Physician. Pour out the healing balm of your Spirit within us; clear our minds and change our outlook so that we may learn to live trusting in you and sharing with others your loving-kindness. Amen.

Desert Journey

Readings: Gen 9:8-15; 1 Pet 3:18-22; Mark 1:12-15

Scripture:
The Spirit drove Jesus out into the desert,
and he remained in the desert for forty days, tempted
by Satan. (Mark 1:12-13a)

Reflection: Without any conscious desire on our part, life brings us into the desert in many ways. It appears in those dreary days and weeks and sometimes years of dry and empty wastes: day after day of nothing but hard work, grief, sickness, emotional and mental fatigue. Maybe that is why we often feel some resistance to entering wholeheartedly into the forty-day desert of Lent with its bleak prospect of facing aridity and testing head-on. We'd prefer to keep fighting that experience as we often fight the deserts of our daily lives—with the distractions of consumerism, hedonism, activism—anything to avoid the desert landscape of our inner lives. But many people have passed through deserts—geographical, intellectual, emotional, and spiritual—and have come out on the other side into a garden of more abundant joy and a deeper peace. You yourself have probably done so more than once!

In Mark's gospel, immediately after Jesus' baptism by John in the Jordan, the occasion of the Spirit's descending on him in the form of a dove, and God's identification of him as God's "beloved Son" (Mark 1:11), the Spirit drives him into the desert. As God's beloved children baptized in Christ we are guided by the same driving force of the Spirit. When Mark's Jesus emerges from the desert, his proclamation is not one of doom and gloom, but of Good News, the "gospel of God!" He is filled to overflowing with the reality of God's reign of love and eager to let us know that that reign is here! Our trip through this year's Lenten desert is a journey with and in Christ. Our enduring belief and trust will bring us through the desert with him into a place of deep and enduring conviction that God's reign of love is here. In Christ we will have the strength to keep on through the barren patches, trusting with him in the bread and water, the guidance and power, the love that is God's gift of God's Self, God's reign of love, to us. This then will be our gift in Christ to others.

Meditation: In what ways are you going through a desert at this time in your life? Reaffirm your faith in Christ's presence in his Spirit and listen for God's word to you.

Prayer: Desert-dweller Jesus, when we are hungry, thirsty, weary, and despairing, renew our hope in God's love for us as beloved children in whom you live. We pray in your name. Amen.

Christ in the Least

Readings: Lev 19:1-2, 11-18; Matt 25:31-46

Scripture:
"Amen, I say to you, whatever you did
for one of these least brothers [or sisters] of mine, you
did for me."

. . .

. . . "Amen I say to you,
what you did not do for one of these least ones,
you did not do for me." (Matt 25:40, 45)

Reflection: "Disciples live lives of service among the marginal nobodies, in opposition to the hierarchical world of exploitative and self-serving power and in imitation of Jesus" (*The New Interpreter's Study Bible*). This assertion emphasizes the radically challenging, even frightening, demands we read from the Gospel of Matthew today.

Life in Christ is not about serving others from a position of self-conscious superiority but about sharing our lives and goods with one another as equals in easy interchange. When giving to others is so natural for us that we do not give it a second thought, we are serving Christ. When we are so preoccupied with clutching our goods and lives to ourselves that we do not even notice others in need around us—individuals, families, political and ethnic groups, we are shutting out

Christ. The generosity of the Gospel is demanding and it has consequences. If we habitually fail to see Christ now, and quite "happily" leave him or her standing in hunger, nakedness, sickness, poverty, prison, outside our circle, why would we want to include her or him at the end of time? Yet, who of us as communities and nations can claim that we have fully renounced this "world of exploitative and self-serving power"? That is the "bad news" we need to face.

The "good news" is that the unself-conscious, totally generous and self-giving love of God lives in us in Christ. Jesus jars us out of our complacency today, but only so we will recognize what is possible if we depend on God's love. With that love we can persevere in our efforts toward personal generosity, and toward making our local and global neighborhoods places where all share the world's resources. God's love will flow through us in our joyful willingness to share our lives fully with one another.

Meditation: Where in your life does generosity arise spontaneously? Where are you stingy in thought, word, or deed? Pray for the grace to love your neighbor as Christ.

Prayer: Christ Jesus, you live in the least as well as in the greatest. Pour out your Spirit in us so that distinctions of economic and social class, differences of race and religion no longer prejudice our responses. Let gracious and mutual receiving and giving become second nature to us. We pray with confidence in your transforming love. Amen.

Prayer of the Heart

Readings: Isa 55:10-11; Matt 6:7-15

Scripture:
Jesus said to his disciples:
"In praying, do not babble like the pagans,
  who think that they will be heard because of their many
      words.
Do not be like them.
Your Father knows what you need before you ask him."
    (Matt 6:7-8)

Reflection: Prayer is not a matter of many words but of the heart. The biblical meaning of heart has to do not just or even especially with affection and emotion, but with our deepest will. The divine lover searches our hearts ceaselessly for any least response to his or her infinite and insistent, yet delicate and sensitive offer of love. Day and night the life-giving, healing energy of the divine Spirit who is Love reaches out from within the center of the universe and the center of each being. It comes in wave upon wave from the endless depths of outer space. It breaks through uniquely in each "yellow tulip" and in "blue iris" (allusions to Denise Levertov's "A Yellow Tulip" and Mary Oliver's "Praying"), in sand dunes, typhoons, baboons, and Minnesota loons. There is no place where you can be, no place that you can see, no place imaginable where divine Love is not.

Prayer is simply letting our wills turn the way they are by nature and grace inclined—to that infinite good of God's Love. It is allowing the vibrations of our lives to be synchronized with the vibrations of the divine dimension in which we live, the risen Christ. For this you do not need a lot of words; you really don't need any—just an inner expectant or affirming glance; a gentle turn of the heart; a deep breath that means "Yes!"; a quiet tear that reveals your hidden desire; a gut release of frantic grasping for control, letting the weight of life shift to the One who wants to bear it for you. This is possible in any trillionth of a second. Each of these, and any of a thousand varieties of other inner and outer barely perceptible movements, is an opening to that Love reaching out to you.

How freeing to hear Jesus today saying, "Don't babble on in prayer, just be simple, be brief! There is no need for impressive words or forced feelings. God knows what you need even before you ask!"

Meditation: Take some quiet time alone. Get in touch with your desires. Notice and accept each of the various things, people, and conditions that arouse in you any kind of desperate desire or cause you to fear their loss. Then, as you are able with God's help, give these gently to God in the words Jesus teaches us saying, "Thy will be done."

Prayer: Gracious God, you know what we need. Grant that to us according to your will and our ability to respond. We pray in you, Jesus. Amen.

Jonah's Second Chance

Readings: Jonah 3:1-10; Luke 11:29-32

Scripture:
While still more people gathered in the crowd, Jesus said
    to them,
  "This generation is an evil generation;
  it seeks a sign, but no sign will be given it,
  except the sign of Jonah." (Luke 11:29)

Reflection: No sign for you, you rebellious ones, no wonder-
working to compel you to faith in God, only the sign of
Jonah, the reluctant prophet. Jesus' words to us may sound
off-putting, but the sign he focuses on suits us very well.
Jonah's story is one with which we can identify.

When God called Jonah to preach repentance to the Nin-
evites, deadly enemies of the Jews, he in essence responded,
"Not me," and headed off in the opposite direction. Like
Jonah, most of us are not eager to invite our enemies to join
in and share the goods of our lives, even the spiritual good.
We head off in another direction until something stops us
up short. Maybe not a literal storm at sea in which we are
thrown overboard, swallowed by a fish, and confined in its
dark belly until we repent and take on the mission God in-
tends for us. But often it takes some kind of storm to bring
us to that point in life and prayer where, confined in inner

darkness, we realize we are totally helpless and turn to God. At that point we, with Jonah, can say: "Down I went to the roots of the mountains; / the bars of the nether world / were closing behind me forever. . . ." There our hearts break open in trust, and as we open to new life, we say with Jonah: "But you brought my life up from the pit, / O LORD, my God" (Jonah 2:7). We begin now to identify with the lost and distressed! Just as God's mercy includes us even at our weakest and in our darkest hour, so it also includes those we have dismissed as unworthy. In compassion we turn and start reaching out to them. Like Jonah we have a second chance to respond to God's call to be inclusive.

Meditation: Recall some way in which your life's journey has been like that of Jonah. In what way, if any, did that experience expand your ability to include and share the good news of God's love with "the other," "the stranger"?

Prayer: God of all nations and all people, bring us through the darkness of sin and suffering to a deeper, more inclusive love of you and all our sisters and brothers. We pray in you, Jesus, in whose dying and rising we are brought into the fullness of life. Amen.

God's Gift in Each Moment

Readings: Esth C:12, 14-16, 23-25; Matt 7:7-12

Scripture:
Jesus said to his disciples:

. . .

"If you then, who are wicked,
    know how to give good gifts to your children,
    how much more will your heavenly Father give good
        things
    to those who ask him." (Matt 7:11)

Reflection: Luke gives a slightly different take on this saying that we hear from Matthew today. Matthew says that if we know how to give good gifts to our children, the bread and fish mentioned in the previous verses, how much more God will give "good things to those who ask" (Matt 7:11). Luke declares that God will give the Holy Spirit to those who ask (Luke 11:13). Both assert God's irrevocable desire to give us what is good; Luke emphasizes that God is not satisfied with giving us good things, but wants to give us God's Self!

God's gift of divine goodness is never withheld from us, but is ours for the asking in each present moment. Sometimes we miss it because of the shadows that conceal it. At the beginning of his spiritual classic *The Sacrament of the Present Moment* Jean-Pierre de Caussade reflects on the fact that Mary was never deluded by God's "shadow which was nothing less than the duties, the demands and the suffering of each moment." These shadows, in fact, "far from deluding Mary, replenished her faith in [the one] who never changes." Because Mary's faith clung fast to God in each present moment, no matter how concealed the divine loving presence, she was ready to give a wholehearted "yes" to that presence in the defining moment of her life, the Annunciation / the Incarnation.

In everything that happens moment by moment, God is present and acting. Most often we see only the shadows—sometimes bright shadows of delight, other times dark shadows of boring routine or relentless suffering. Every shadow, as de Caussade points out, is a sacrament of the divine presence. There is no secret to finding God there. We have only "to carry out faithfully the simple duties of a Christian and of [our] condition, humbly to accept the suffering involved and to submit without question to the demands of Providence in everything that is to be done and suffered."

Meditation: What circumstances and events of your daily life are sacraments of God's presence and action?

Prayer: Hidden God, you are the infinite richness, beauty, and goodness hidden beneath the surface of every day's duties and demands, behind the veil of its refreshing moments and hours of rest, within the energy of its creative acts and just beyond the dead weight of tension and dread. Help us to accept the content of every moment just as it is with faith that welcomes you hidden beneath the surface. We pray in gratitude. Amen.

Life-giving Looks

Readings: Ezra 18:21-28; Matt 5:20-26

Scripture:
Jesus said to his disciples:
"I tell you,
   unless your righteousness surpasses that
   of the scribes and Pharisees,
   you will not enter into the Kingdom of heaven."
      (Matt 5:20)

Reflection: "If looks could kill . . . !" Though I do not know the origin of this much-used phrase, the assumed ending is that you and I and many others would be long dead—probably after many murders of our own! Imagine what would happen if thoughts could kill. We'd probably be living in a sparsely inhabited world! I don't really know, of course, but I am aware from observing my own "thoughts," that they are punctuated with various-sized dark clouds of negative judgments and dismissive attitudes about other individuals and groups.

Righteousness in Scripture has to do with relationships. In today's gospel reading Jesus is telling us that being "right" with God and others is about more than carrying out the external aspects of the law. It is about living in harmony with them from the inside out. Righteousness certainly includes our actions, the dimension stressed by the scribes and Pharisees. But, says Jesus, it also has to do with our words and attitudes. We do not share God's reign of love fully if we speak to and about others in ways that are demeaning or dismissive, or if we harbor hateful and destructive attitudes about them. Christianity is a matter of the heart as well as of actions.

Today's gospel challenges us first to be aware of our intentions and attitudes, and of our speech, and then to change. No part of this is easy—not facing ourselves honestly, nor letting go subtle and habitual inner negative attitudes. It is not even possible without God's help, which, of course, is always and superabundantly available in the Spirit of Christ who loves us just as we are. When in the words of the psalm response we plead, "Out of the depths I cry to you, O LORD," (Ps 130:1a), we share the trust of the psalmist that in infinite kindness God will graciously free us from our iniquities (Ps 130:7-8). Then "seeing" the God who is love (see Matt 5:8), "our looks will not kill," but bring life.

Meditation: In what ways are you being invited to let your inner attitudes as well as your words come into right relationship with particular other individuals and groups?

Prayer: Patient God, you never tire of looking on us with kindness and love. Help us be aware of the negative ways we look at ourselves and others. In your generosity please grant us the grace to be changed by your loving gaze so that we may look at others with that same love. We pray in the Spirit of Christ who is Love. Amen.

Loving Enemies

Readings: Deut 26:16-19; Matt 5:43-48

Scripture:
Jesus said to his disciples:

. . .

"[B]ut I say to you, love your enemies,
   and pray for those who persecute you,
   that you may be children of your heavenly Father,
   for he makes his sun rise on the bad and the good,
   and causes rain to fall on the just and the unjust."
      (Matt 5:44-45)

Reflection: "Nobody can keep you from loving," a wise person once remarked to a friend of mine. Inclusive love that goes out even to our enemies is possible for us. This is hard to believe, and difficult to live. How can we love those who hate us? That includes the coworker who gossips about us, the neighbor who snubs us, the sister or brother, ex-wife or husband who has refused to speak to us for years. Our first response to them is not usually, if ever, positive regard! Most often we would like to have them out of our lives. But God has never stopped loving them. Divine Love reaches out to all in sunshine and rain, loving "the bad and the good" (Matt 5:45). This Love lives in you and me.

As children of God we share the divine DNA, the spiritual genetic instructions that gear our lives toward mercy and compassion that image God's being and life. Every day Divine Love is on the move, wanting to reach out from within our own basic core of goodness, to touch others and reveal to them their own basic core of goodness. As Christians through faith and baptism we open and commit ourselves to that Divine Love. That Love can free us from whatever barriers are keeping us from loving our enemies—weariness, fear, greed, hatred, resentment, pain, hopelessness—whatever narrowness of mind or smallness of heart keep the warmth and refreshment of divine Love from shining on our alienated sisters or brothers. The reign of God is here and it is freely poured out within and around us. To access it we need only turn around to welcome it, trusting in our own basic goodness and that of all our brothers and sisters in whom the gracious gift of God's Spirit in Christ lives.

Meditation: As you notice yourself judging others or wishing them harm, turn in faith to Christ's Love within; as you are able, choose to breathe it out to them.

Prayer: Transforming Love, touch our hearts and change our minds as only you can. Help us know your love so that we can freely let go our hatreds and prejudices, no matter how we have been hurt. Show us how to share your love. This we ask in the Spirit of Christ who is Love. Amen.

Listen and Live

Readings: Gen 22:1-2, 9a, 10-13, 15-18; Rom 8:31b-34; Mark 9:2-10

Scripture:
Then a cloud came, casting a shadow over them;
  from the cloud came a voice,
  "This is my beloved Son. Listen to him." (Mark 9:7)

Reflection: Only recently have I become acquainted with the "bog people," some of whose corpses have been found more or less intact in the bogs of Ireland and northern Europe. Researchers have conjectured that at least some of these people may have been human sacrifices. It is not surprising that in today's first reading Abraham hears God asking for the offering of his son Isaac as a holocaust. This story from an era about two millennia before Christ reflects a belief common to the consciousness of many cultures: only the sacrifice of a human person would be fitting worship of God. What is surprising is the break through in human consciousness that comes with Abraham's understanding that though God wants his total devotion, God does not want him to kill his son to demonstrate that.

    God is a God of life, not of death. God does not want us to kill ourselves or others for God's sake. God does not want us to die but to live. Jesus comes to open our awareness fully to this wonderful reality. God is pouring out all the divine life in Jesus, the Christ, and through him to and in us so that with him we can give our lives to God with all our heart, mind, soul, and strength. This is the only fitting expression of that divine self-gift that lives in us. Our self-gift includes our every thought, word, and action, and it includes our dying—because that is our way into the fullness of life in the resurrected Christ. Paul tells us in the second reading: "It is Christ [Jesus] who died—or, rather, was raised—who also is at the right hand of God, who indeed intercedes for us" (Rom 8:34). Paul's turn of phrase is telling: God gives us life not only through Christ's dying but primarily, or "rather," as he says, by Christ's being "raised." In Jesus' transfiguration today we celebrate the glory of divine life in him that will be ours with him as God's "beloved" forever in the risen life of Christ. Let us "[l]isten to him" (Mark 9:7) and live!

Meditation: In a quiet place read and reread today's gospel slowly several times with the intention of calmly, trustingly, and intentionally opening to the gifts of Christ-life pouring out in you. Then simply listen to God repeating this phrase in your heart: "You are my beloved." After some time respond in whatever way you wish.

Prayer: God of Life, fill us with your life in Christ as we live in hope for eternal life through our dying and rising in him. Amen.

March 9: Monday of the Second Week of Lent

Compassion

Readings: Dan 9:4b-10; Luke 6:36-38

Scripture:
"But yours, O Lord, our God, are compassion and
    forgiveness!
Yet we rebelled against you
    and paid no heed to your command . . ." (Dan 9:9)

Reflection: "Poor thing! She is so pitiful!" Sometimes we make comments like that about a neighbor or acquaintance who has fallen into hard times and doesn't seem to be able to find relief, someone who, perhaps, cannot let go a feeling of resentment about life's injustice, or who seems caught perpetually in some grief. Our comments may come from a superior attitude. We cannot understand why this person does not rise above what seems like a self-defeating attitude and move on with life as we have. We may feel pity, but not really compassion.

Compassion is more than feeling sorry from an objective or superior position for one who is suffering or in trouble. Being compassionate is to have some experience of what it is like to suffer what the other suffers. According to Phyllis Trible, the original meaning of the Old Testament word "compassion" is "trembling womb." Compassion is a gut feeling for someone. It connects us to them physically, psychologically, and spiritually. It is a feeling that also drives us to do what we can to alleviate another's suffering (see Michael Downey, "Compassion," in *The New Dictionary of Catholic Spirituality*). Without over-identifying to the point of inability to support another, our compassion makes us able to hear another person's cry of pain, knowing in our gut what the other might be feeling. Because of that, we are willing to take action to help, even if that action can only be staying with another in the suffering.

God is compassionate. We are made in God's image and likeness. Compassion is in our genes, in our souls. The shape of the divine compassion that is meant to permeate our lives is not only shown us in the life and teaching of Jesus; Jesus activates it in us by taking our suffering and death up into his, and so allowing our lives and deaths to be permeated by the compassionate Spirit of God. In Christ dying and rising within us, we are able to do as today's gospel invites: stop judging, stop condemning, forgive and give, like our heavenly Mother/Father who is compassionate.

Meditation: Take some time to sit quietly and welcome yourself and your life just as it is with compassion. Now think of someone or group you tend to judge harshly. Welcome them into your imagination, and as you are able, look at them with compassion.

Prayer: Compassionate God, you know what we suffer. Thank you for looking on us with kindness and pouring out your Spirit in us so that we can be kind and compassionate to ourselves and others. We pray in Jesus who is the human expression of your compassion. Amen.

March 10: Tuesday of the Second Week of Lent

Willingness

Readings: Isa 1:10, 16-20; Matt 23:1-12

Scripture:
If you are willing, and obey,
   you shall eat the good things of the land . . . (Isa 1:19)

Reflection: Quite a long time ago I heard a recording of the comedian Bill Cosby imitating the verbal tussles he and his brother had as kids. His brother was accusing him of eating all the Jell-O in the refrigerator. Bill's comeback was "Who made you the Jell-O sheriff?" Sometimes we think and act like the Jell-O sheriff, or maybe even like the boss-of-everything!

In his book *Will and Spirit: A Contemplative Psychology* the late psychiatrist and spiritual teacher Gerald May plumbs the distinction between "willingness" and "willfulness." The difference, he says, is not easy to explain; the two sometimes overlap. Willingness always includes an inner trusting attitude of "yes" to the deep and positive spiritual energy of life that is bigger than ourselves. As religious people we connect that energy with the divine, which creates, sustains, and moves the universe and everything in it. As Christians we recognize in it the Spirit of Christ. Willfulness, on the other hand, is the exercise of our autonomous ego power over some thing, person, or circumstance—even over ourselves. It may or may not be in harmony with a deeper willingness.

For example, I might tear the door of a house down to rescue someone from a fire: a willful act rising out of a deep willingness. Or I might break in to rob my neighbor of his computer: a willful act disconnected from the deeper God-energy of life.

Today, in a special way, Christ in our midst in Scripture, liturgy, and life is pleading with us to grow in willingness, that is, to get in tune with the positive energy, the love of God that is ours for the turning. Jesus advises us in the gospel reading to let go our drives to be teacher and master. Stop, he says, "ty[ing] up heavy burdens" for yourselves and others "to carry." Let go the compulsion to make yourself or others do and be what your short-sighted vision has in mind. Instead, tune into your life's deepest energy, the Holy Spirit, grace, and let it guide you in helping yourself and others to carry "[life's] burdens" (Matt 23:4).

Meditation: Take some time today to tune into the deeper desires of your heart. Let yourself know them, and as you are able, entrust them to the stream of the Spirit's life and energy within you.

Prayer: Christ Jesus, your willingness to live in harmony with God's will was total. Through your Spirit free us from our ego-driven harsh willfulness so that we may live and act with the supple strength of that same willing Spirit. Amen.

March 11: Wednesday of the Second Week of Lent

Servant Leadership

Readings: Jer 18:18-20; Matt 20:17-28

Scripture:
But Jesus summoned them and said,
. . .
"[W]hoever wishes to be great among you shall be your
    servant;
  whoever wishes to be first among you shall be your slave.
Just so, the Son of man did not come to be served but to
    serve
  and to give his life as a ransom for many."
        (Matt 20:27-28)

Reflection: Servant leadership has become a common phrase since Robert K. Greenleaf's book *Servant Leadership* popularized the notion some thirty years ago. Since then many programs, courses, institutes have sprung up to foster leadership as service. Jesus' teaching and example predate these by hundreds of years and are the inspiration for many. Jesus teaches us in today's gospel reading that life is not about achieving powerful positions; it is about living and acting with integrity that respects one's own gifts and is motivated by desire to use them to help others.

In his life as servant, Jesus neither sought nor refused public notice. He was not driven by the need to please others—

nor to displease them. Rather, with integrity he embraced his hidden life in Nazareth and later the public life in which he freely shared his gifts as an influential preacher, teacher, and healer. Even in the face of opposition he spoke out boldly and courageously the Good News of God's reign of love present for all, rich and poor, neighbor and stranger, sinner and saint, sick and well. He was not a social, religious, or political climber focused on riches and prestige or on control over others. He never used force to dominate or badger others into accepting his viewpoint. The powerful effectiveness of his life and message came from his generous acceptance of himself just as he was, the embodiment of God's infinite well of love. This he offered freely to all. His was a life of total harmony between his divine and human gifts fully expended for others' good.

The Spirit of the risen Christ Jesus lives on in our lives, making available to us the same integrity, trust, generosity, and courage. Whether behind the scenes or in the public forum, we are invited to use our unique gifts in service motivated by Christ's love in us.

Meditation: What ego projects, whether material or spiritual, are you being asked to drop? What use of your gifts, motivated by loving service, to consider?

Prayer: Gracious God, you have given us Jesus to show us how to live and serve with humility, courage, and integrity. Help us to follow his example, depending on his Spirit. Amen.

"Both Sides Now"

Readings: Jer 17:5-10; Luke 16:19-31

Scripture:
Blessed is [the one] who trusts in the LORD,
    whose hope is in the LORD.
He is like a tree planted beside the waters
    that stretches out its root to the stream:
It fears not the heat when it comes,
    its leaves stay green;
In the year of drought it shows no distress,
    but still bears fruit. (Jer 17:7-8)

Reflection: Some of us oldies remember the Joni Mitchell song "Both Sides Now." With the songwriter we've gazed at clouds, relationships and love, work and all the challenges of life not only from above and below but from every angle. And often with Mitchell we conclude that we still do not understand life at all. Many of our experiences are hard or impossible to understand; they are ambiguous, unclear, uncertain, confusing! People who hope in God do not always appear to be planted beside running streams, full of vigor, and bearing fruit! Sometimes they look bereft, befuddled, and defeated!

Take Lazarus in today's gospel reading! Our first glance at him does not reveal a tree whose leaves are green or that seems to be bearing fruit. Rather, Lazarus is like a tree that is languishing, withering, and dying of malnutrition, disease, neglect! Was he or was he not trusting in God? Was he trusting too much in the rich man instead of God? Or maybe, though he appeared desiccated, diseased, and starved, he was "still full of sap, still green." That is what we come to see in the last part of the gospel reading—he was fruitful at a level beyond what our senses can fathom in his earthly life at the rich man's gate. Because his heart remained fixed in God through all his adversity, his life hidden in God continued to flourish and he was filled with comfort even in and after death.

When we look around at life, at ourselves, at others, it is important to remember that appearances can be illusions. When we or others look like winners, we may be losers; when we look like losers, we may be winners. The determining factor, trust in God, is not always obvious. Life by that running stream of divine life and love is at a level perceived only by the eyes of faith. It is, however, available to all who are willing to plant their roots near that river of grace by opting to trust and to keep trusting no matter what life brings: ups or downs, giving or taking, winning or losing.

Meditation: Look around at your neighborhood and world. Let go harsh judgments and open your heart to the poor and the rich. Pray that all of us may be like trees finding the stream of God's life, stretching out their roots to it.

Prayer: God of the poor and God of the rich, turn our hearts together to trust only in you so that we may drop our attachments to material wealth and freely share all that we are and have. Amen.

Envy and Jealousy

Readings: Gen 37:3-4, 12-13a, 17b-28a; Matt 21:33-43, 45-46

Scripture:
Israel loved Joseph best of all his sons,
    for he was the child of his old age;
    and he had made him a long tunic.
When his brothers saw that their father loved him best of
    all his sons,
    they hated him so much that they would not even greet
      him. (Gen 37:3-4)

Reflection: When one of my grandnephews became a big brother to his first little sister, his response to his mother's getting ready to leave the hospital with the new baby was, "Do we have to bring her home with us?"

"To be green with envy" captures the nauseating feeling that arises when someone else is threatening our position as number one. Childhood competition and rivalry follow us into our adult lives as spouses, parents, neighbors, bosses, and coworkers. The desire to be esteemed and loved for who we are with our unique talents is deep within all of us, and we are all prone to feel that the love or acclaim given to someone else means that we are unloved and rejected. There may be times we are like Joseph's brothers, hating the person who seems to prefer another. Having these feelings does not mean we are bad persons! Of course, acting them out is sinful. Even that sin, as we know from the Joseph story and from Jesus' own story, can be forgiven!

Awareness of feelings of jealousy, envy, and hatred provides a special moment of grace. Each time we honestly and compassionately accept these painful emotions is an occasion to turn intentionally to the loving, intimate presence of God in the Spirit of the risen Christ. Christ knows what it is to be rejected, unloved, ignored, and passed over. And he knows the freedom, the self-forgetful love, the peace, joy, and well-being that come from intimacy with God, and trusting ultimately that only divine, unconditional love satisfies. In him that intimacy is possible for us; feelings of jealousy, envy, and competition can be our doorways into ever deeper experiences of that intimacy in which our competitive feelings and attitudes melt away.

Meditation: Get in touch with some rivalry, envy, or jealousy you feel. Allow it into your awareness and let it be. Then turn to the divine loving presence within you and rest in that love embracing you in your unique goodness.

Prayer: O God, your love alone satisfies our deepest needs. Help us to acknowledge our fears of not having or getting enough. Transform our fears into gateways into your personal love for us. We pray in Jesus' name. Amen.

God's Longing for Our Return

Readings: Mic 7:14-15, 18-20; Luke 15:1-3, 11-32

Scripture:
So he got up and went back to his father.
While he was still a long way off,
  his father caught sight of him, and was filled with
    compassion.
He ran to his son, embraced him and kissed him.
  (Luke 15:20)

Reflection: Years ago when Henri Nouwen was in our area, he presided at Eucharist in our monastery chapel on the Third Sunday of Advent. The theme of his homily, as I remember, had to do with the joyful expectation characteristic of that season and Sunday. The example he used came out of his experience of much travel around the world. He commented that as he was arriving at an airport, it was always an occasion of excited expectation for him when he knew he would soon be spotting a friend or family member in the waiting area waving a welcome over the crowd and coming toward him exclaiming, "Yoo-hoo, Henri! Over here!" No matter who we are, it is comforting to know that there is someone waiting for us, eagerly hoping for our return.

The spendthrift son of today's gospel would probably not have been thinking along those lines. After all, he left his father, mother, brother, and home in a rebellious and independent mood. "Just give me my share, thank you; I can manage on my own very well without you!" His father, however, never stopped looking and longing for his return. We can imagine him gazing every day toward the horizon or the distant hills—even walking out beyond the nearest bend to see if, just maybe, today he is coming home.

Jesus assures us that this is how God thinks about us. Even if we have tried to sever our relationship God never gives up on us. The first reading also reveals a God who is our shepherd, one who does not "persist in anger," but rather "removes guilt," "delights . . . in clemency," and "cast[s] into the depths of the sea all our sins," a God of "faithfulness" and "grace" (Mic 7:18-20). God is a loving, compassionate father; God is a gentle, tender mother who never forgets us (see Isa 49:15.) We can take courage and return; God is out eagerly scanning the horizon for the first glimpse of us coming back home.

Meditation: Are there ways you have tried to sever your relationship with God? Have you thoughtlessly wandered away? Are there ways you are being invited to return? How do you imagine God to be, to feel toward you?

Prayer: Ever-watchful and caring God, thank you for being on the lookout for our return. Give us the trust to run with eagerness toward your outstretched arms. We pray in union with Jesus, your beloved. Amen.

March 15: Third Sunday of Lent

God's Temple

Readings: Exod 20:1-17; 1 Cor 1:22-25; John 2:13-25

Scripture:
While he was in Jerusalem for the feast of the Passover,
    many began to believe in his name
        when they saw the signs he was doing.
But Jesus would not trust himself to them because he
        knew them all,
    and did not need anyone to testify about human nature.
He himself understood it well. (John 2:23-25)

Reflection: Jesus was not naive. He knew that we can easily be swayed by signs and wonders, and that we might very well prove unreliable when the road gets narrow and tough. We can sometimes be seduced by the highs in life: a little glory feels good, and an unexpected jackpot at the casino gives us a rush of adrenalin. Nothing wrong with those things, but we can easily allow the pleasure they bring to become addictive, and we start to live, if not for the next acclamation or windfall, at least the next affirmation. If there is someone around who looks like she or he can make it happen, we are drawn to throw our lot in with him or her. Jesus didn't need anyone to point this out to him. "He himself understood it well" (John 2:25b). Jesus knows human nature from the inside out with all its temptations to go after the quick dollar, the front-page splash, the top position! The Synoptic Gospel writers point this out to us in their accounts of Jesus' own temptations in the desert. However, Jesus' total dependence on the God-life in him kept him from succumbing in the same way the temple salespeople and money-changers in the gospel had done, and in the ways we do.

Jesus knew his own human nature with all its weaknesses—and all its strengths, most particularly the strength of its total openness to the divine life within him. Today Jesus captures our attention by clearing our lives of the clutter and confusion of compulsive drives for gain and glory. "You've got your priorities wrong!" he says. "I am God's temple, and so are you because you live in me. God's house is not a place for mercenary competition! Stop putting excessive energy into material and spiritual glitter and gold, setting your hearts on signs and wonders. Trust in the abiding strength of God that lives in all life's goods, even its most devastating experiences through my dying and rising." The riches of God dwell in this temple of your life now and will forever in the heavenly temple.

Meditation: Remembering that you are God's temple, let yourself become aware of any unnecessary inner or outer mercenary business or clutter that Jesus is inviting you to let go.

Prayer: Jesus, you are God's temple, and in you we share that privilege. Help us let go whatever keeps us from being houses of prayer open to God's presence and action within us. In your Spirit we pray. Amen.

March 16: Monday of the Third Week of Lent

Hope and Healing

Readings: 2 Kgs 5:1-15b; Luke 4:24-30

Scripture:
. . . [V]aliant as he was, [Naaman] was a leper.
Now the Arameans had captured in a raid on the land of Israel
   a little girl, who became the servant of Naaman's wife.
"If only my master would present himself to the prophet in Samaria,"
   she said to her mistress, "he would cure him of his leprosy." (2 Kgs 5:1-3)

Reflection: "Hope," God says in Charles Péguy's poem by the same name, is "a little girl." Hope says her prayers every night, goes to bed and sleeps well, rises with the morning, meeting each day with a fresh outlook, greets poor people and orphans. She is like a bud, the promise of springtime, the pledge that better times and renewed life are coming.

"Valiant as he was," Naaman would have had no hope for the cure of his leprosy except for a "little girl, who became the servant of [his] wife" (2 Kgs 5:1, 2). Embodied in that little girl, hope stirred up his attention to new possibilities for his health and wholeness. Even at that he almost missed his chance because he shifted his gaze away from the modest ways in which hope was stirring. He almost got stuck in expectation that new life and restored health could come only from some dramatic intervention. Naaman angrily huffs at the prophet Elisha's directions sent via a messenger: "Go and wash seven times in the Jordan, and your flesh will heal, and you will be clean" (2 Kgs 5:10). He turns his back and walks away saying, "I thought that he [the prophet] would surely come out and stand there to invoke the LORD his God," . . . "move his hand over the spot, and thus cure the leprosy" (2 Kgs 5:11). "What is this washing in the Jordan? It can't be that simple! If it were, I could have washed in the rivers back home," he must have thought. Again it is little people with their quiet, reasonable voices who steer him back to trust that health and wholeness will come to him in a simple way. "[I]f the prophet had told you to do something extraordinary, would you not have done it?" they ask.

The prophetic word of God often comes to touch and heal us through simple people and the ordinary, unremarkable, quiet events of life: the suggestion of a little neighbor girl, the kind word of a clerk or maintenance person, the inspiring words and actions of the carpenter's son who lives down the street.

Meditation: What little voices of hope are calling for your attention?

Prayer: God of hope, you reveal yourself in the little things of life. Open our eyes and make us sensitive to your presence and action in the ordinary places and events of life. Amen.

Forgiveness

Readings: Dan 3:25, 34-43; Matt 18:21-35

Scripture:
Peter approached Jesus and asked him,
  "Lord, if my brother sins against me,
   how often must I forgive him?
As many as seven times?"
Jesus answered, "I say to you, not seven times but
     seventy-seven times." (Matt 18:21-22)

Reflection: Alexander Pope, the English poet, said it first, but we have all heard it many times: "To err is human, to forgive divine." God cannot help forgiving. The Latin word from which our English word "forgive" takes its origin is *perdonare*, which means to give fully, completely. That is God's nature, to give God's Self fully. "God is love" (1 John 4:8b). Love's nature is to be effusive, to pour itself out completely to, for, and in others, holding nothing back. This dynamism of Divine Love is not motivated by our worthiness, but rather by the immense generosity that is its nature. God forgives, gives totally, even when we have offended, betrayed, or attacked God directly or in others.

  In Scripture and celebration of sacraments God is with us in Jesus Christ giving food, health, good news, love, acceptance, and helpful challenge. He consoles us when we are sick, forgives us when we have wronged someone, includes us whether we are poor or rich, women or men. Ultimately Jesus gives his life to us in his dying, rising, and pouring out of his Spirit.

God's love in Jesus includes every one of us no matter who we are or what we have or have not done, no matter what condition we are in. Among his dying words to God on our behalf is his consoling prayer as he dies, "Father, forgive them, they know not what they do" (Luke 23:34a). Just as those whose hatred or indifference put Jesus to death did not know what they were doing, neither do we really know what we are doing when we hate, are indifferent, or refuse to forgive ourselves or others. We do not know how deeply such withholding of love goes against the flow of the divine life within us, our baptismal life. The Spirit of God longs to pour out love through us, giving and forgiving. With our graced consent this is possible. "To err is human"; to forgive is also human, as well as divine.

Meditation: Remember the presence of Christ's forgiving love in you; spend some time in quiet letting your body and spirit relax. Let someone who needs your forgiveness come to mind. Say "I forgive you," or if you are unable, ask God for the grace to do so.

Prayer: Forgiving God, keep our hearts expanding in your love so that we may generously extend forgiveness to others. We pray in your Spirit. Amen.

Fulfilling the Law

Readings: Deut 4:1, 5-9; Matt 5:17-19

Scripture:
Jesus said to his disciples:
"Do not think that I have come to abolish the law or the
    prophets.
I have come not to abolish but to fulfill." (Matt 5:17)

Reflection: Following Jesus means radical conversion, not
only exterior conformity to law but a change of heart. Jesus'
declaration that he comes not "to abolish but to fulfill" (Matt
5:17) alerts us to listen up and find out what he means.

In the Sermon on the Mount, chapters 5 through 7 of Matthew's gospel, Jesus as the new Moses interprets the law for
us, his followers, in a way that uncovers its interior dimension. Obeying the law at this deeper level, Jesus says, will
make us great in the reign of God; it will "bless" us with
"seeing God" by making us "clean of heart" (Matt 5:8).

In the gospel section following today's reading, Jesus ex-
pands on what obeying means. Don't toss out the obvious
external requirements, he says, but take a look at the law's
more subtle demands. Not to murder stands as a fundamen-
tal moral pillar. But it includes giving up angry and insulting
words and thoughts (see Matt 5:22 ff.). Later on Jesus declares, "from the heart come evil thoughts, murder, adultery,

unchastity, theft, false witness, blasphemy. These are what defile a person . . ." (Matt 15:19-20a). In contrast to the Pharisees, Jesus emphasizes the radical interior dimension of God's reign. At the end of his public ministry, Jesus says, "cleanse first the inside of the cup, so that the outside also may be clean" (Matt 23:26).

The gospel calls us not only to freedom from exterior acts of lying, stealing, cheating, killing, greed, gluttony, and adultery but also to freedom from the evil inclinations of the heart in which they begin. No matter what their biological, psychological, or social origin, such destructive thoughts and feelings arise within us as part of our human condition. Our humanity in Christ is also illumined and strengthened by his loving Spirit so that we have the light to see them, the compassion to accept them, and the courage to let them go. Fulfilling this interior dimension of the law is our path to happiness.

Meditation: During your prayer time reflect on areas of your life where external conformity with the commandments is not matched by your interior disposition. Ask the Spirit of Christ to give you the interior freedom to allow your life to be more integrated and your actions more authentic.

Prayer: Purify our hearts, O God, so that we may live not only in external conformity with your law but in the interior freedom to act out of love. We pray in your Spirit. Amen.

Joseph the Builder

Readings: 2 Sam 7:4-5a, 12-14a, 16; Rom 4:13, 16-18, 22; Matt 1:16, 18-21, 24a or Luke 2:41-51a

Scripture:
   [Jesus'] mother said to him, . . .
"Your father and I have been looking for you with great
      anxiety."
And he said to them, . . .
"Did you not know I must be in my Father's house?"
      (Luke 2:48-49)

Reflection: Jesus claims God as his Father, calling the temple his "Father's house" (Luke 2:49). Mary also calls Joseph his father (Luke 2:48). Joseph was a good role model for Jesus, a trustworthy mirror of God his Father.

   Joseph's identity as a carpenter is found only in Matthew's gospel. People in the synagogue at Nazareth ask in amazement, "Is he not the carpenter's son?" (Matt 13:55). In Mark's gospel Jesus himself is called a carpenter by the people of Nazareth (Mark 6:3). The Greek word used in both places is *tekton*, which can mean carpenter, but can also refer to other builders who work with hard materials such as stone or metal.

   God is the great *tekton*, the master builder of the universe and of the earth. Joseph's life as a carpenter in Nazareth imaged God's creative work in a way his growing "son" could understand and imitate. Joseph showed the young Jesus how to be a skilled builder. The qualities of a good carpenter helped shape Jesus' spiritual building in his public life. He had an eye for good material. It could be flawed but full of potential. Preaching, teaching, and healing, Jesus had a firm but gentle hand guiding the saw, lathe, and plane of his Spirit. He knew whether or not a sharp edge was needed. Sanding was necessary, but not to be overdone. Just as he was able to put a piece of new furniture together, Jesus was able to unite people in creative ways that enhanced their goodness and made them capable of serving a higher purpose.

God in the risen Christ continues to build the earth as tectonic plates shift, forming and re-forming our planet. In Christ, God also shapes and reshapes our personal and community lives. Jesus the carpenter is building a beautiful and welcoming home. Trusting the work of his sensitive and caring Spirit, we can be builders too.

Meditation: How is God at work in you, in your family, and community, building something new?

Prayer: Master-Builder God, you shape and reshape our world. Help us be sensitive to your subtle shaping and reshaping of our lives through the work of your Son, Jesus. Amen.

God Lovable and Loving

Readings: Hos 14:2-10; Mark 12:28-34

Scripture:
I will heal their defection, says the LORD,
  I will love them freely;
  for my wrath is turned away from them.
I will be like the dew for Israel:
  he shall blossom like the lily . . ." (Hos 14:5-6)

Reflection: The gospel today focuses on the great commandment—loving God above all and loving one's neighbor as oneself. No religious practice tops that in importance. In fact, every religious practice, whether of worship or asceticism, has to do with cultivating and expressing love. God's commandment of love is not intended to squelch life, cut short our joys, deprive us of life, or make us crumble in guilt; it is intended to open our eyes to the reality that God is loveable and loving, and we ourselves, and others, are loveable and capable of loving. To be loved and to love is our human vocation, and only that will make us happy.

God is good, we are good. That reality is the foundation of life. Think of the beginning in the book of Genesis not as past, but as ever present. The Source of our being is with us now! In this ever-present beginning, God, the fountain of life, is creating the heavens and the earth, the sun, moon, stars, all the plants, flowers, and animals, woman and man—in God's image and likeness. And God looks and says, "Wow! This is really good! I love it!"

We who are made in God's image and likeness share in that divine goodness. It is ours to receive and give. Along life's ways, though, we "defect" (Hos 14:5) from the way of love for lots of reasons—genetic, social, psychological, spiritual, moral. Because of the tough experiences in life, and sometimes because of easy access to too much of everything, we grow out of touch with the one thing that is most important—God's deep love for us and in us. We may then lose confidence in our own basic goodness as a gift from God uniting us to others in love. We may allow our minds to become narrow, our hearts bitter, and our souls small. We may get caught up in fighting with our neighbors for resources, recognition, or power. Even our sin, however, and all our failures are part of the greater mystery of creation, redemption, and transformation in Christ, a journey into a greater freedom to receive and give God's love. God is always "heal[ing] [our] defection, [and loving us] freely" (Hos 14:5).

Meditation: How has God's goodness and love touched you today, this week, this year? How do you feel called to respond in love?

Prayer: Infinite Love, your goodness never ends. Turn us back to you so that we may rejoice in your goodness now and forever. We pray in Christ. Amen.

The Dawn of New Life

Readings: Hos 6:1-6; Luke 18:9-14

Scripture:
"Let us know, let us strive to know the LORD;
   as certain as the dawn is his coming,
   and his judgment shines forth like the light of day!
He will come to us like the rain,
   like spring rain that waters the earth." (Hos 6:3)

Reflection: Hope comes with dawn, new life with the spring rain. Most of us have spent some sleepless nights anxious about or despairing of some possibility for our life or another's: a future for a child caught in addiction, a long and peaceful retirement with a spouse now sick, a career that just vanished with failure to meet academic standards, our own ability to be generous and loving. Such a restless, oppressive night seems endless, and even the thought of the coming dawn brings no relief. These nights of seeming hopelessness extending into days and weeks do not go unnoticed by God who is always with us in the Spirit of Christ. God keeps saying, "Keep looking for me! Watch for my coming in your darkness." "[A]s certain as the dawn is [my] coming," and my light will "shine forth like the light of day" for you. "I will bring fresh new blessings into your life," just as does the "spring rain that waters the earth" (Hos 6:3).

The tax collector in today's gospel may have lost hope, specifically in his own ability to be "righteous," that is, to live justly and lovingly without the gift of God's mercy and loving-kindness in his life. But he never gave up hope in God. He "return[ed] to [God]" as Hosea invites us to do (Hos 6:1). Knowing his place, he "stood off at a distance," put all his trust in God and "prayed, 'O God, be merciful to me a sinner'" (Luke 18:9). Our nights of waning hope in ourselves and our ego-strength's ability to achieve whatever we will can open us to that deeper interior divine help coming from within and beyond us. Humbly accepting our human needs and relying on God for help will bring us to the exaltation of new life.

Meditation: In what ways has losing hope in your own ego-focused accomplishments helped you find your place "at a distance" and turn to God for the merciful help you need?

Prayer: God of mercy and kindness, you come like the dawn into our deepest darkness. Open our eyes in trust so that we can rely on your goodness rather than our own power or privilege. We pray as tax collectors and sinners. Amen.

Truth

Readings: 2 Chr 36:14-16, 19-23; Eph 2:4-10; John 3:14-21

Scripture:
Jesus said to Nicodemus:
> "Just as Moses lifted up the serpent in the desert,
>   so must the Son of Man be lifted up,
>   so that everyone who believes in him may have eternal
>   life."

. . . [W]hoever lives the truth comes to the light,
>   so that his works may be clearly seen as done in God.
>   (John 3:14-15, 21)

Reflection: "Truthiness," a word coined by political satirist Stephen Colbert on Comedy Central's *Colbert Report*, is bandied about by many with humor, as we assess the political scene. It refers to ideas, convictions, opinions, based on gut feelings alone, not on researched facts or sound reasoning. Feelings can help guide us to the truth, but they can also be wrong. In the middle of a dark night alone in a cabin we may be sure a creaking sound is someone pushing open the door, only to realize in the morning that it is a loose tree branch blowing in the wind. Finding truth is not easy. Feelings can mislead, research is never complete, reasoning can falter, intuition fails. Patient, persistent exercise of our whole being in search of truth—gut, mind, and heart—is necessary, but even then we can be mistaken.

"What is truth?" Pilate asks when Jesus tells him that he has come into the world "to testify to the truth" (John 18:37-38). Jesus does not answer Pilate, but he has addressed that question earlier in the Fourth Gospel. More than a gut feeling, more than an idea or rational conclusion, truth is a person to whom and in whom "we belong." The truth to which Jesus testifies is the loving presence of God in Jesus. He in fact says, "I am . . . the truth . . ." (John 14:6). We know Jesus, the Truth, by believing in him, that is, saying "yes" to him with our whole being—body, mind, emotions, spirit—through the power of his Spirit. The Truth who is Christ cannot be fully grasped with our minds but can be embraced by love. In him we live the truth and come to the light so that "[our] works may be clearly seen as done in God" (John 3:21). Jesus is the Truth in whom we live and act, and who lives and acts in us.

Meditation: Make an act of faith in Christ's presence. Repeat interiorly, "You are the Way, the Truth, and the Life."

Prayer: Infinite Truth, present with us in the Spirit of Christ, draw us more deeply into you so that with ever-expanding hearts and minds we may live and act in our world as authentic expressions of your truth, even though you are always beyond our total understanding. Amen.

Creating Something New

Readings: Isa 65:17-21; John 4:43-54

Scripture:
Thus says the LORD:
Lo, I am about to create new heavens
   and a new earth;
The things of the past shall not be remembered
   or come to mind.
Instead, there shall always be rejoicing and happiness
   in what I create . . . (Isa 65:17-18a)

Reflection: "Make way! Get ready! Watch this! I am about to make something new!" How excited God sounds. "You," s/he says, "will be so amazed at what I am going to create, you will not even think about things past. This is going to be a source of everlasting joy and happiness. You just wait and see!"

Out of the darkness and chaos of Genesis, God breathes and speaks creation into being—water, earth, sky; sun, moon, stars, and planets; fish and birds; vegetation of all kinds; animals and flowering plants and trees, woman and man in God's own image and likeness. Creation continues on the move from that beginning, which is not only in the past but in the present, deep within all that exists now. And it beckons us on from the outer reaches of the future. In Jesus' historical life God's connection with all creation was revealed, and in his dying and rising his Spirit permeates all creation. In Christ and through the leaven of his Spirit, God is creating and re-creating, shaping and reshaping the universe and all of us.

In our poor bruised earth and in each of our vulnerable embodied spirits, susceptible in our present state to sickness and sin and destined for death, divine creation manifests as healing, which is sometimes physical, sometimes psychological, sometimes spiritual—but always healing of some sort whether before, in, or after death. Healing can come, however, only with our desire, our consent, and our cooperation, when we want it as much as the royal official of today's gospel. Today we can come to Jesus with him saying, "Sir, come down before my child dies" (John 4:49). "Sir, come before I die, before we kill each other. Come before we lose hope, before we destroy our world. Create something new out of the suffering and chaos in our lives, out of the darkness of our hearts and minds, out of the injustices in our world. And as you will and we are able, put us to work as creators and healers with you."

Meditation: Today quietly allow yourself to become aware of your desire for healing for yourself or another. In your heart let Jesus know what you need and want.

Prayer: Creating, healing God, you are pouring out the balm of your Spirit in our bodies and spirits and in our world. Please deepen our desire for wholeness in you, and increase our capacity to bring your healing Spirit to others. We pray in you, Jesus. Amen.

Water of Life

Readings: Ezek 47:1-9, 12; John 5:1-16

Scripture:
>. . . I saw water flowing out
> from beneath the threshold of the temple toward the east;
. . .
[The angel] said to me . . .
"Wherever the river flows,
> every sort of living creature that can multiply shall live,
> and there shall be abundant fish,
> for wherever this water comes the sea shall be made
>   fresh." (Ezek 47:1, 8, 9)

Reflection: The feel of warm, soothing water gently washing over our tired bodies after a day of hard work renews and refreshes us. A glass of cold water in the middle of a hot day quenches our thirst and restores our spirit. The gentle lapping of waves on the shore of a nearby river or lake on a dark night as we rest securely in cabin or tent lulls us into peaceful sleep. Our bodies are composed mostly of water. At birth we emerged from the waters of our mother's womb just as our animal ancestors came up out of the womb of the sea eons ago. We continue to look for planets where there is water, because where water is, there is life. Our physical lives depend on water; our psyches are immersed in the flowing waters of every day's stream of consciousness as well as in the symbolic ocean-depths of our unconscious; our spirits depend on the cleansing, refreshing water of God's Spirit. Water, the womb of life, can also be its tomb. Raging floods at times cause havoc and destruction. The biblical Red Sea that parted to save the Israelites in their Exodus is the same water that destroys the Egyptians, their oppressors.

Water fills today's readings. Ezekiel's temple river brings freshness and fruit wherever it flows; John's pool of Bethesda provides stirring waters to heal the blind, sick, and lame. Both are images of the Spirit of the dying-rising Christ who alone fulfills the promise of the temple stream and the Bethesda pool. "Wade in the Water," urges the traditional spiritual. That invitation grabs us at many levels. Today's readings invite us to wade into the symbolic water of baptism, immersing ourselves in Christ's dying and rising so that the creating, re-creating river of God's life fills us. Cool your brow, quench your thirst, and soak your tired feet; float, swim, dive, and splash in the healing, sin-destroying, life-giving Water of Life, the Spirit of Christ.

Meditation: At various times during the day use your imagination to immerse yourself in the refreshing, life-giving water of God's Spirit.

Prayer: O infinite, life-giving Stream, you continually pour out your Spirit in our lives and world. Guide us as you will to your banks and beaches to immerse ourselves in you so that we may be renewed in your Spirit. In Christ we pray. Amen.

Like Mary

Readings: Isa 7:10-14; 8:10; Heb 10:4-10; Luke 1:26-38

Scripture:
The angel Gabriel was sent from God
    to a town of Galilee called Nazareth,
    to a virgin betrothed to a man named Joseph,
    of the house of David,
    and the virgin's name was Mary. (Luke 1:26-27)

Reflection: The Renaissance painter Giovanni "Bellini [had] it wrong," about the way the annunciation took place, says poet Kilian McDonnell, OSB. Bellini, along with many artists, medieval and modern, paints a serene Mary caught up in prayer in the temple as a powerful, winged angel descends gracefully into her lovely, silk-and-velvet-clad presence, inviting her to participate in the mystery of the Incarnation.

But Mary was an ordinary, poor, Jewish young woman, probably not more than thirteen or fourteen years old—a marriageable young adult in her time and culture. She was not a weak, shy and retiring, housebound lady as we know from Scripture. Cooking, cleaning, bringing in wood, and carrying water from the public well to her extended family's home, with its simple, few rooms surrounding a modest courtyard, would have been part of her daily routine. She was tough enough to travel by foot and donkey during her pregnancy through

rough hill country to visit her cousin Elizabeth, and then from Nazareth in the remote north all the way to Bethlehem in the south where she gave birth in an animal shelter.

As the poet suggests, Mary was probably at home doing her daily chores when the Holy Spirit invited her in some mysterious way to bear Jesus. Mary's strength of body is matched by her vigor of spirit. She engages God actively in her questioning, "How can this be . . . ?" (Luke 1:34). She must have known the kind of unbelieving resistance and accusations she would hear from family and neighbors if she agreed to this strange-sounding plan. Wrestling with the implications for her life and the lives of her loved ones, she gave a wholehearted, "Yes!"

The Holy Spirit also comes to us ordinary people not only when we are in our Sunday best, kneeling recollected in prayer, but when we are right in the middle of life, just as it is with its daily grind, its demanding and sometimes confusing circumstances. While we, like Mary, struggle honestly with our doubts and misgivings, God lovingly waits for our courageous "Yes!"

Meditation: Whenever you change from one activity to another today, or stop to answer door or phone, direct your attention to the Holy Spirit addressing you.

Prayer: Is that you, gracious God, greeting me in the knock at the door, the words of a neighbor? Help me know to what you are inviting me, so that like Mary I can say "Yes!" I pray with desire to be open to your Spirit. Amen.

Wanting to Come

Readings: Exod 32:7-14; John 5:31-47

Scripture:
"You search the Scriptures,
   because you think you have eternal life through them;
   even they testify on my behalf.
But you do not want to come to me to have life."
      (John 5:39-40)

Reflection: God has had it with the golden-calf-worshiping Hebrews, seemingly severing identity with them, calling them "your people" instead of "my people," and declaring, "I will make you, Moses, a great nation instead of them!" (see Exod 32:7-10). Was Moses, as biblical scholar Carroll Stuhl-mueller asks, "projecting *his own* problem into the mind of God?" Maybe Moses in his frustration wanted to be rid of the burden they were and so imagines God would want that, too. But another part of Moses trusted God to forgive and remember the pledge that they would become "as numerous as the stars in the sky," and inherit the Promised Land (Exod 32:13). Moses haggles on their behalf, and God relents.

Jesus, in today's gospel passage, is frustrated with the people who will not recognize him as the one sent by God in spite of all the testimony given through John's witness, his own works of healing, and the Scriptures. Jesus tries to show them their error by energetically pointing out all the compelling evidence that he is the one they have been looking for.

God wants to stay with us, his wayward people, and Jesus continues his diligent efforts to manifest God's presence to us who are slow to believe. However, we can only experience it now if, as Jesus says, we "want to come to [him] to have life" (John 5:40). Watching for signs, hearing the testimony of others, and searching Scripture with our intellects are important, but not enough. Even they can become false gods. Only loving desire that goes deeper than any concept will open us to God in Jesus and fill us with lasting life.

Meditation: Today notice whatever is taking you away from appreciation of God's presence in others' lives, in Scripture, or in your own life. Renew your desire to find God in and beyond all things.

Prayer: Gracious God, you always want to come to us. Stir up our desire to come to you; guide us to see your presence in the people and events of our daily lives, but not to mistake them for you, who are always beyond our comprehension. We pray in Jesus through his Spirit. Amen.

The Hour

Readings: Wis 2:1a, 12-22; John 7:1-2, 10, 25-30

Scripture:
. . . [T]hey tried to arrest him,
but no one laid a hand upon him,
because his hour had not yet come. (John 7:30)

Reflection: The anxiety and the joyful anticipation of an important hour—the hour of giving birth, the hour for an important exam or interview, the hour of our wedding, of a loved one's dying, of our own death—such an hour can dominate our consciousness. In John's gospel, Jesus speaks frequently about "his hour." When at the wedding at Cana, Mary tells him the couple has run out of wine, he says what has that to do with me for "[m]y hour has not yet come" (John 2:4). Jesus speaks to the Samaritan woman about the "coming hour" when all "true worshipers will worship the Father in Spirit and truth" (John 4:23). John tells us today that those who tried to arrest Jesus at the feast of Tabernacles were unable to "because his hour had not yet come" (John 7:30).

The meaning of this mysterious hour for Jesus becomes clear when, after his final entry into Jerusalem accompanied by the joyous crowds waving palm branches—the prelude to his betrayal, death, and resurrection—he says to his disciples, "The hour has come for the Son of Man to be glorified" (John 12:23). Jesus' hour of dying and rising is at once the most excruciating and the most fruitful and glorious experience of his life. It is the hour that gives meaning to every other hour of his life and ours.

In his last talks with his disciples, Jesus compares his hour and their hour of losing him in death to that of a mother giving birth:

> When a woman is in labor, she is in anguish because her hour has arrived; but when she has given birth to a child, she no longer remembers the pain because of her joy that a child has been born into the world. So you also are now in anguish. But I will see you again, and your hearts will rejoice, and no one will take your joy away from you. (John 16:21-22)

Whatever we suffer in the "hours" of life, if we surrender all into the great "hour" of Christ's dying and rising, we will, ultimately, if not immediately, know the joy of his risen presence, and "no one will take [our] joy away from [us]" (John 16:22).

Meditation: What "hour" are you anticipating with dread, joy, anxiety, eagerness? Remembering Christ's presence with you in his dying and rising, entrust that hour to him.

Prayer: Ever watchful God, open each of the hours of our lives to the joy and challenge of your life-giving presence in Jesus' dying and rising. We pray in him through the Holy Spirit. Amen.

Believing

Readings: Jer 11:18-20; John 7:40-53

Scripture:
Some in the crowd who heard these words of Jesus said,
"This is truly the Prophet."
Others said, "This is the Christ."
But others said, "The Christ will not come from Galilee,
will he?"

. . .

So a division occurred in the crowd because of him.
(John 7:40-41, 43)

Reflection: "[T]hese words of Jesus" refer to his declaration in the previous passage that "[w]hoever believes in me, as scripture says: / 'Rivers of living water will flow from within him'" (John 7:38). John then comments that Jesus was talking about the Holy Spirit who would be given through his death and resurrection to believers (John 7:39).

Most of the speakers in today's gospel had not come as believers and so were not filled with the rivers of living water, the Holy Spirit. Some of them were saying this about Jesus; some that; still others something else. Each speaker seemed to have an opinion about his origin, or about the way his words and actions fulfill or do not fulfill Scripture. But they could not agree; they got stuck in their own limited viewpoints. Each had a piece of information, but they did not and could not, of themselves, know everything there is to be known of Jesus, no matter how careful and thorough their investigation. Nevertheless, most seemed quite certain about the opinions they had formed based on limited knowledge. All, that is, except the uneducated temple guards and Nicodemus, the educated Pharisee. They, on the other hand, are more open-minded, saying in essence, "Wait, listen to him; do not immediately condemn him without first hearing him!"

We are probably quite a bit like these people of Jesus' historical lifetime—not totally transformed by faith. We know certain things about Jesus from our study of Scripture and theology. From time to time we may argue about who he is or is not. Since none of us has all the answers, we would do well to take the advice of the temple guards and Nicodemus: go to him in faith and listen. What we cannot know fully from our own efforts he will reveal to us in an intimate personal way in prayer receptive to his Spirit.

Meditation: Take time today to set aside your thoughts, judgments, and opinions about Jesus or anyone else, including yourself; repeat trustingly, slowly, quietly, interiorly: "Come, Holy Spirit!"

Prayer: Come Holy Spirit, strengthen our faith so that in Scripture, sacrament, and life we may hear Jesus' words and know his actions in a way that transforms us. Amen.

March 29: Fifth Sunday of Lent

Seeing Jesus

Readings: Jer 31:31-34; Heb 5:7-9; John 12:20-33

Scripture:
Some Greeks who had come to worship at the Passover
    Feast
    came to Philip, who was from Bethsaida in Galilee,
    and asked him, "Sir, we would like to see Jesus."
        (John 12:20-21)

Reflection: "Let me see, let me see!" I remember pleading
quite often as a small child, especially when I thought my
older sisters or brothers were looking at something I hadn't
seen yet! Often I'd get a response puzzling to me, "There is
no see (sea!) to it; it's all dry land!"

Today's request by the Greeks to see Jesus while they were
in Jerusalem for Passover seems quite a normal one, one to
be expected in light of Jesus' growing reputation for preaching, teaching, and healing, "Sir, we would like to see Jesus"
(John 12:21). They, I imagine, expected a direct response. But
when Philip, the one they asked to introduce them, goes with
Andrew to let Jesus know about it, Jesus gives quite a mysterious answer—nothing as straightforward as "Tell them to
come!" Instead he advises them that "unless a grain of wheat
falls to the ground and dies, it remains just a grain of wheat

. . ." (John 12:24). Today we have the same request they did: we want to see Jesus. And we get the same response.

The gospels are written from a postresurrection perspective. John shapes this incident or story recalled from Jesus' historical life to teach those who heard this gospel in the early church how they could "see" Jesus. And he is teaching us. Seeing Jesus is more than a matter of physical sight. It has to do with faith, that is, with a loving, trusting relationship. That faith relationship unites us "like a grain of wheat" with Jesus in his death so that in and with him we "[produce] much fruit" (John 12:24). Jesus realizes that this is the only way we are really going to "see" him as he is. To know him in love by surrendering our lives and deaths into his living and dying will open our inner eye of faith to his ever-loving, glorified, and glorifying presence (John 12:23, 27).

Meditation: Read and slowly reread today's gospel passage. As you are drawn to do so, close your eyes and open your inner eyes of faith; repeat in prayer whatever response rises in your heart.

Prayer: Divine Eye, we believe in you who live in us and open our inner eyes to your light. Increase our faith so that we may see you more clearly at work in our world. We pray in Jesus, the risen Christ, who is "the light of the world" (John 8:12). Amen.

The Drama Within

Readings: Dan 13:1-9, 15-17, 19-30, 33-62 or 13:41c-62; John 8:1-11

Scripture:
. . . [T]he scribes and the Pharisees brought a woman
who had been caught in adultery
and made her stand in the middle. (John 8:3)

The assembly believed them [the two wicked elders],
since they were elders and judges of the people,
and they condemned her to death. (Dan 13:41b)

Reflection: A crowd of people out early in the morning at the temple to hear Jesus; two women accused of adultery—Susannah clearly innocent, the woman of the gospel, guilty as far as we know; two lecherous elders taking revenge on Susannah for her refusal; a gullible assembly of the people ready to sentence Susannah to death; some crafty scribes and Pharisees trying to trick Jesus into revealing himself either as a harsh judge or as a law breaker; the wise, discerning, and courageous Daniel who finds a way to let the wicked old men fall into their own trap. This cast of characters crowds around us at today's Eucharist. Drama on every side—the good guys and gals versus the bad gals and guys. In these stories that we have heard often we know who will emerge with life and limbs intact, saved at the last moment by a noble hero's courageous intervention!

At today's Eucharist this jostling crew comes alive again in our hearing and in our inner lives. We know the endings of these stories, but the struggles and tensions they depict are still going on in our lives between ourselves and others, or inside our own heads and hearts. Sometimes it's hard to know who is on what side! Whether we are innocent, like Susannah, or guilty like the woman of the gospel, will a hero emerge to save us? We live on with the tension, the drama continues. But today's gospel assures us that Jesus, just and merciful, is with us and that he understands all the characters of our outer and inner lives in all their complexities. He remains deeply calm within us, calling our attention firmly but gently to our own sins and shortcomings, gazing on us with love, inviting us to change, but never condemning us. His quietly heroic, saving Spirit rises from within and around us to make this possible.

Meditation: Get in touch with the thoughts and feelings jostling within you. Are you worrying about being judged, or hardening your heart in unforgiving condemnation of another? Invite Jesus into these feelings and tendencies and listen to him.

Prayer: Gracious God, all your judgments are true and all your will is love. May Jesus, the risen Christ within us, turn our hearts to you. In him free us from condemning ourselves and others. Through his and your Spirit we pray. Amen.

March 31: Tuesday of the Fifth Week of Lent

Spiritual Food

Readings: Num 21:4-9; John 8:21-30

Scripture:
. . . [W]ith their patience worn out by the journey,
  the people complained against God and Moses,
  "Why have you brought us up from Egypt to die in this
      desert,
  where there is no food or water?"
We are disgusted with this wretched food!" (Num 21:4-5)

Reflection: These sentiments uttered by the travel-weary
Hebrews on their Red Sea road as they continued their seemingly endless trek to the Promised Land often echo our own.
By this time in Lent, maybe in life, we could be tired of keeping on with "this wretched food" to sustain us. What in the
beginning seemed like interesting work, enriching relationships, challenging ascetical practices, fruitful connections,
exciting possibilities for a life or a Lent with God in prayer,
all has turned to sand and ashes. We feel trapped in the same
old self, duties, faces, and things to do; yes, even things to
eat! If only there was something more appetizing than this
manna! Something about being in the middle of a long journey, the middle of a job, and the middle of life is wearisome
and frustrating. How we moan and grown and grumble.
Why can't life be like it used to be? We want those onions,

those leeks, a little garlic, at least something to spice things up! But there is no going back, and now we know we will not make it to the end on our own steam. That's good!

Now is the time to stop, acknowledge our dissatisfaction, and give ourselves a rest from murmuring and trying too hard. It is time to realize the limits of what the goods of this world can give and what we can achieve on our own steam and to look for the food that is being given at the spiritual level of our being. This job, this practice, this kind of prayer, this food, good as they are—none of these things of themselves can satisfy us, no matter how hard we try to make them. But with the psalmist we can pray in the words of today's responsorial psalm: LORD, hear my prayer; / let my cry come to you. / Do not hide your face from me / now that I am in distress" (Psalm 102:2-3). Then in our misery, as we look to Jesus, "the Son of Man lifted up in death and resurrection" (John 8:28, paraphrase), we will realize the truth of his guarantee to us that "I am the bread of life" (John 6:48). Jesus is the life-giving food we need on our journey.

Meditation: What are you grumbling about? Repeat this prayer slowly and trustingly: "Hear my prayer in my distress."

Prayer: Only in you, God, do our souls find rest. Help us enjoy life's goods and accept its insufficiencies and our own inadequacies with equanimity and grace as we look to you for the food we need, Christ Jesus, who is our Life. Amen.

Remaining in Christ

Readings: Dan 3:14-20, 91-92, 95; John 8:31-42

Scripture:
Jesus said to those Jews who believed in him,
  "If you remain in my word, you will truly be my disciples,
  and you will know the truth, and the truth will set you
    free." (John 8:31-32)

Reflection: In today's gospel reading, Jesus is asking "those Jews who believed in him," and us, to "remain in [his] word" so that [we] will "know the truth, and the truth will set [us] free" (John 8). The community for which John wrote was a late first-century group of mostly Jewish Christians who were experiencing growing tension between Judaism and Christianity. By then the realization of Christ as divine was becoming much clearer. This truth, a seeming contradiction of Jewish monotheism, was precipitating an agonizing decision for them. To remain in Christ's word (John 8:31) would mean continuing in their commitment to him as that divine risen presence in their lives in spite of being excluded from the synagogue, their religious home and that of their friends and neighbors (see Sandra M. Schneiders, *Written That You May Believe*).

This Scripture was for them, as it is for us, more than a flat, one-dimensional account of some past event or teaching inviting intellectual consent. Its symbolic words bring to light THE Living Word, Christ present, speaking and acting in life. In the words of John's gospel, Jesus was inviting this early Jewish community to let go any obstacles to their commitment to him—old ways of thinking and acting—so that they could be free to let the truth of his personal risen presence permeate their lives. This was a time for them to experience how radical the change required by this commitment, a time of great purification, but also of enlightenment.

Lent is a special time of purification and enlightenment for us also as catechumens prepare for baptism and all of us ready ourselves for recommitment to our baptismal life. Christ here in our midst in scriptural Word and sacrament invites us to accept him as the Light of our lives (John 8:12), not just in intellectual assent, but in an embrace of love. Remaining in Christ in love and celebrating and intensifying that relationship in prayer and sacrament will be to "know the truth" that "set[s us] free" (John 8:32).

Meditation: Pray for the light to know more clearly how you are called to commit yourself to Christ, and for the strength to let go whatever you need to in order to do that.

Prayer: Loving God, enlighten our minds and purify our hearts so that we may accept more fully our baptismal grace, Christ the Light of our lives living in us his Body. We pray in his name. Amen.

April 2: Thursday of the Fifth Week of Lent

I AM Your Life

Readings: Gen 17:3-9; John 8:51-59

Scripture:
Jesus said to them, "Amen, amen, I say to you,
    before Abraham came to be, I AM."
So they picked up stones to throw at him;
    but Jesus hid and went out of the temple area.
        (John 8:58-59)

Reflection: At the end of today's gospel passage Jesus clearly identifies himself as "I AM." That is the mysterious name God gives to Moses when the Israelites press to know who is sending him to lead them out of Egypt. (See Exod 3:13-14.) Imagine throwing stones at God, the great I AM while God hides. A strange scenario!

But it may not seem so strange if we remember that the people of Jesus' historical life would hear a claim like that as blasphemy protesting: "Who does this young upstart think he is, not yet fifty years old, claiming to be God, the I AM that existed before Abraham!" They would quite understandably have thought they knew who he was: a country boy from the north, part of an uneducated, working-class family! All they heard about or even experienced of his persuasive preaching, teaching, and healing seemed incongruous.

John is writing from a postresurrection perspective, at the end of the first century. He and his community had grown deeply into awareness of the spiritual presence of the risen Christ permeating their lives with his enlightening and healing power in the Holy Spirit. Transformed by this faith experience, they were able to articulate more clearly their belief, which John puts into words. His words uncover that same faith experience going on in our lives and communities.

Over and over again in John's gospel, Jesus invites our response to his risen presence as the great I AM. "I am," he says, hidden among you, always remaining beneath the surface, waiting to fill your inner being as "the bread of life" (6:35), "the light of the world" (8:12), "the gate" (10:7, 9), "the good shepherd" (10:11), "the resurrection and the life" (11:25), "the way and the truth and the life" (14:6), "the true vine" (15:1). If you are hungry, if you are in darkness, shut in, closed off, lost, dying on the vine; if you are uncertain, confused, without sap, desiccated and brittle, don't throw stones. Turn interiorly and come to me; I am your life.

Meditation: With confidence ask Christ Jesus to let you know his presence as the source of your life and all life.

Prayer: Infinite I AM, help us see and rejoice in your being manifested in all the wonderful particulars of creation, ourselves too. Free us from our too ready tendency to throw stones; turn our minds and hearts to look for the good. Amen.

God's Work

Readings: Jer 20:10-13; John 10:31-42

Scripture:
Jesus answered them,

. . .

"If I do not perform my Father's works, do not believe me;
but if I perform them, even if you do not believe me,
believe the works, so that you may realize and understand
that the Father is in me and I am in the Father."
(John 10:34, 37-38)

Reflection: "The proof is in the pudding." Our common understanding of that proverb's meaning is that we cannot know the true worth of something or someone by claims made, but only by performance. Jesus tells the people that even if they do not believe what he is saying, they could know who he is by his work because it is the work of God.

The work of God is the work of love. From the beginning God pours out divine goodness in creating light and darkness, earth and sea, fruit trees and plants, sea creatures and birds, beasts and cattle, women and men. God's ever-active loving work frees and saves the Israelites from slavery. In John's gospel, Jesus is saying, "Yes, God created and saved through the divine word and work in times past, and God is speaking and acting now in and through the Divine Word and work. I am that Word (see John 1:14); I am doing the work of God, re-creating, healing, and freeing you."

John opens our eyes of faith to God's work in Jesus by singling out seven special signs: the transformation of water into wine at Cana, curing the royal official's son by life-giving word alone, healing the paralytic at the pool of Bethesda, multiplying loaves and walking on water, giving sight to the man born blind, raising Lazarus from the dead. The transforming life-giving power of each of these signs foreshadows God's great work of love in John's eighth and greatest sign, THE SIGN, Jesus' dying, rising, and pouring out of the Holy Spirit.

The work of God in us is to "believe in the one [God] sent" (John 6:29). That means entrusting ourselves—body, mind, soul, spirit—to him in his dying and rising. In baptism and Eucharist we celebrate that work transforming us, making us able to do the work of God in daily life.

Meditation: Pray for the grace to believe God's work of love, Christ dying and rising in yourself and others. Join in the great "Amen" of the Eucharist, the great sign of that work.

Prayer: Divine Worker, you are at work in our world in Christ. Make all our work part of his dying and rising so that your love for and in us and others may bring unity and peace. Amen.

At Home in God

Readings: Ezek 37:21-28; John 11:45-56

Scripture:
Thus says the Lord God:
I will take the children of Israel from among the nations
   to which they have come,
    and gather them from all sides to bring them back to
      their land. (Ezek 37:21)

Reflection: In a world in which many women, children, and men are exiled from their homelands because of war or desperate political and economic circumstances—think Iraq, Darfur, Mexico, Somalia, Cambodia, Korea, Vietnam—Ezekiel's words are comforting. He was prophesying from Babylon during the time of the Israelite captivity in the sixth century before Christ. He spoke with confidence of a new day, a new covenant in which God's people would be restored to their land and worship in a new temple. Even though we may be living in our country of origin, we may still know the exile of inner alienation. Unfortunate separation from loved ones through divorce or death, loss of job or reputation, or seemingly irresolvable conflicts can leave us lost and distant from ourselves and those we love. We know the feeling of wanting to go home—back to our own land, the place we were safe and at peace.

Historically there was a return by the Israelites to their land. Ezekiel was right about that. But his words bear more than that limited reality. The "gathering" of "the children of Israel" "from all sides to bring them back to their land" (Ezek 37:21) is a theme taken up again by John in today's gospel reading. He says that when Caiphas the high priest advises killing Jesus so that the death of one will save the nation from Roman captivity, he was unwittingly declaring that Jesus' death would not only save the nation but also "gather into one the dispersed children of God" (John 11:52). We are the dispersed children of God, lost and alone when we are out of touch with our deepest selves where God lives in the Spirit of Christ, and when we are separated by negative, destructive thoughts and actions from our neighbors and friends.

Why must Jesus die so that we can be gathered as God's children back into our own home, life in God? Only by lovingly knowing and accepting us at our worst, lost, burdened, gone astray with our hatreds and hostilities, can God in Jesus bring us to the deepest realization that we are loved. No matter our circumstances, our attitudes, our inadequacies, God's Love, the Holy Spirit, is drawing us into God, our lasting home.

Meditation: Are there ways in thought, attitude, or action that you have left your home in God? Remember God's total acceptance of you as you are and open your heart to Christ's loving Spirit.

Prayer: You, O God, are our eternal home. Thank you for welcoming us and all people into your unconditional love. We pray in Christ through his Spirit. Amen.

A Human God

Readings: Mark 11:1-10 or John 12:12-16; Isa 50:4-7; Phil 2:6-11; Mark 14:1–15:47

Scripture:
[Christ Jesus] emptied himself,
   taking the form of a slave,
   coming in human likeness;
   and found human in appearance,
   he humbled himself,
   becoming obedient to the point of death,
      even death on a cross. (Phil 2:7-8)

Reflection: Jesus' triumphant entry into Jerusalem and his passion reflect our own story. Watching Mark's drama play out in our imaginations is like seeing our lives unfold.

Most of us are eager to show up and participate when things are going well, as are the cooperative disciples and exultant crowds at Jesus' entry into Jerusalem. Their disbelief that they could betray Jesus lurks in our hidden defenses, protecting us from our own capacity for treachery. The overwhelming weariness of the Gethsemane disciples overtakes us in times of sorrow. Our self-assured, loud protestations of loyalty to death are likely to crumble like Peter's in the face of threats to our own safety and life. We want to run away like the disciples when our lives, our jobs, our reputations are in danger. Later we regret and weep over our failures like Peter. We are willing to spend our resources lavishly for someone we love and are about to lose, like the woman who pours expensive ointment over Jesus' head. We stay with someone we love through suffering and death as did the gospel women, and with the courage of Joseph of Arimathea we claim our association with the outcast and despised. Whatever our human weaknesses and human strengths they will impinge on others' lives for better and for worse.

Our own human strengths and weaknesses and those of others—the ones we love and who love us, and the ones we do not love and who do not love us—all our human experience is embraced by Jesus in his passion and death. He does not "regard equality with God / something to be grasped" (Phil 2:6). Jesus identifies completely with us to the deepest dregs of human experience, the sense of being abandoned by God. Living in Christ we can trust beyond feeling that we are never alone in suffering or joy. God has taken on our humanity in Christ.

Meditation: Spend some time today quietly reading and rereading some of these Scripture passages. Welcome the way Christ comes into your life through them.

Prayer: Christ Jesus, we are stopped short by silent amazement, in awe of your humility and goodness. Stay with us on our journey through life, strengthening our wills and guiding our words and actions so that fully accepting our own humanity we may be transformed by your divinity. Amen.

April 6: Monday of Holy Week

Servants of Justice

Readings: Isa 42:1-7; John 12:1-11

Scripture:
Here is my servant whom I uphold,
   my chosen one with whom I am pleased,
Upon whom I have put my Spirit;
   he shall bring forth justice to the nations. (Isa 42:1)

Reflection: Jesus is the servant well pleasing to God, the one on whom God's Spirit rests. His service is to "bring forth justice to [all] nations" (Isa 42:1). Justice is a quality of God's nature: "the LORD," as Isaiah says, "is a God of justice" (Isa 30:18). Justice is also characteristic of the divine action: "You are righteous [O God], / and just are your edicts" (Ps 119:137).

Recently, I heard an interview by Margaret Warner of PBS with Swedish lifelong diplomat Jan Eliasson, current United Nations special envoy to Darfur. In it he describes the depressing circumstances of the two million plus displaced people there—the lack of food, clean water, and education, the constant threat and experience of violence. In spite of the slowness of positive action on our part to alleviate this crisis and establish peace, his way of analyzing and addressing the situation reveals his total commitment. Even in his weariness he conveys quiet and strong determination, and complete willingness to use on behalf of peace and justice all his intelligence, experience, education, and diplomatic skills. For me he is a convincing embodiment of God's beloved servant.

From early Christian theology based in the New Testament, we understand that God's nature is relational, a divine community engaged in a constant dynamic of giving and receiving love, each of the Persons of the Trinity joyfully ecstatic in this mutual interchange. God is right relationship. And all God's actions are for the sake of bringing about right relationships in our world, that is, justice. God's primary action in our world is in Jesus, the servant "upon whom," as God says, "I have put my spirit" to "bring forth justice to the nations" (Isa 42:1). This he does for the most part quietly and gently (Isa 42:2-3), but persistently and courageously teaching, preaching, touching, and healing. He never backs off from this, his presentation of himself as Divine Love incarnate and his message of love: the restoration of right relationships among all people in God's reign.

Meditation: How is your life in Christ calling you to be a servant of justice?

Prayer: Jesus, you are God's humble and courageous Servant, willing to give your life so that justice may be restored. Give us the courage and grace to remain faithful to you in our lives of service for the sake of justice. We pray trusting in your Spirit. Amen.

Suffering Servant

Readings: Isa 49:1-6; John 13:21-33, 36-38

Scripture:
Reclining at table with his disciples, Jesus was deeply
    troubled and testified,
  "Amen, amen, I say to you, one of you will betray me."
. . .
When [Judas] had left, Jesus said,
  "Now is the Son of Man glorified, and God is glorified
    in him." (John 13:21, 31)

Reflection: What depths of dread and anguish Jesus felt as
he reclined at table with his disciples. This was their last
meal together on earth. Aware of Judas's treachery, he was
sure that one of his best friends, Peter, would also deny him.
The foreboding as he anticipated total rejection, cruel treat-
ment, and death at the hands of people he loved weighed
down his spirit. Jesus was human; he knew in bones and
brain, gut and heart, nerves and feelings the suffering of a
victimized human being. And yet he says at the end of this
gospel passage that now is the time of his glory!

    This postresurrection viewpoint reflects the early Christian
community's faith experience of Jesus' risen presence in the
Holy Spirit. They know Jesus' brutal suffering and death, and
that through it God's glory and goodness triumphed. Now

as the risen Christ, he lives in them and they in him. Their own life cycles of birth, growth, achievement, pleasure, joy, labor, diminishment, pain, and death are drawn into his living and dying in the Spirit. Their gaining and losing, laboring and resting, rejoicing and suffering, too, will be transformed by God's glory.

Isaiah's Suffering Servant in the first reading foreshadows Jesus as the one through whom God was to show the divine glory (Isa 49:3). Though he thought he had toiled in vain (Isa 49:4), God would make him "a light to the nations," and through him would make salvation "reach to the ends of the earth" (Isa 49:6b). In Christ we participate in this servanthood. No suffering is useless, no labor is in vain. No joy is too trivial, no action to spread the Good News too insignificant, no expenditure of energy too small, no gracious acceptance of diminishing strength too trivial to be an important part of God's work of manifesting the divine glory. Our dying and rising in Jesus is an integral part of his bringing salvation to all.

Meditation: Read slowly today's Scripture passages. Give yourself over to the Spirit through whatever words, images, or silence attracts you.

Prayer: Jesus, you are God's Suffering Servant. Help us to be aware of all the anguish and dread in our lives and world. Unite us with you in your suffering, death, and resurrection so that God's glory may triumph in the salvation of all. Amen.

Night

Readings: Isa 50:4-9a; Matt 26:14-25

Scripture:
When it was evening,
  he reclined at table with the Twelve.
And while they were eating, he said,
  "Amen, I say to you, one of you will betray me."
    (Matt 26:20-21)

Reflection: Evenings and nights are often times for intimacy. Evening may mean time to be comfortably alone with our thoughts, or for reading or writing; it may mean sharing our experiences and feelings with a close circle of family or friends. Night may be a time for playing with one's children, making love, enjoying some entertainment, or spending time in prayer. Most of us look forward to the end of a day, to relaxation, reunion with loved ones around the table, good food shared, and time to reconnect and be renewed in body and spirit, or to be quiet or engage in creative interests. Nights introducing a holiday break, whether they are to be spent alone or with friends, are anticipated with even more than usual joy. Festive meals on the evenings beginning religious feasts usually promise great delight.

But this is not always the case. There are those evenings, those long dark nights when for some reason we are deeply alienated from ourselves or others. We may be fearful, anxious, and preoccupied, worried about someone we love, or some aspect of our life. We may be dreading some news or event. We may be in danger, wracked by pain, or paralyzed by expectations at work or in a relationship. We may be lost in grief, weighed down by failure, disappointment, or betrayal in love, fatigued to the point of nausea and unable to care.

In yesterday's gospel, John described Jesus as "deeply troubled" at the realization that one of his disciples would betray him. Today Matthew says the disciples were "deeply distressed" by the knowledge of Jesus' betrayal by one of them. This happened when "it was evening," while they were eating (Matt 26:20). In John, when Judas left the supper room to execute his plot, "it was night" (John 13:30). The night of these gospels has the feel of emotional and spiritual darkness, turmoil and desolation in the face of evil that cannot be avoided. This was Jesus' experience. And it is sometimes ours. He knows well what we experience and stays with us through our nights to bring us with him to resurrection and a new day.

Meditation: Remember the nights of your life—peaceful and troubled. What will the coming night be? Unite it intentionally with Jesus' experiences of night—both joyful and terrifying.

Prayer: Praise to you, God. You make "us glad as many days as you humbled us . . ." (Ps 90:15). In trouble we trust with the psalmist that when "weeping comes for the night," "at dawn there [will be] rejoicing" (Ps 30:6b).

A Note about the Triduum

Triduum refers to the time from the evening of Holy Thursday through Easter Sunday Evening Prayer. It is one ritual celebration in three movements, the greatest feast of the year for Christians. During this protracted single feast we slow down in order to immerse ourselves ritually into the great saving event of Christ's life, death, and resurrection. We gather for the liturgies as one people of God, not so much to hear and dramatize the past, but to enter more fully into the actual event of Christ's living, dying, and rising now in our lives and communities, and to welcome new Christians into the depth of this experience in baptism, confirmation, and full participation in Eucharist. When we gather to hear Scripture and to celebrate these sacraments, we are drawn more intensely and deeply into Christ's dying and rising. Stretching the one "day of salvation" out for three days to ritualize it carefully and attentively allows us to be purified and illumined by the divine life that lives in us and in which we live.

On Holy Thursday we assemble as one community united in the one loaf of Christ's Body given and the one cup of Christ's Blood poured out in self-giving love. We ritualize this self-giving love by washing one another's feet, by presenting gifts for the poor along with the bread and wine to be offered in Eucharist, and by receiving the gift of his Body and Blood, which will nourish us and give us the strength to love one another. As we leave, we begin a period of silence and fasting that will open us interiorly to the great mysteries we are celebrating.

On Good Friday we walk with Christ in his dying, entrusting to him our own dying to our false selves, our losses in life, and our actual physical dying. We share in his sorrow, his suffering, his sense of abandonment, but also in his absolute trust in God through this great darkness. The passion narrative draws us not only into Christ's being "lifted up" on the cross in death but also into his being "lifted up" in Resurrection. We pray not only for ourselves but for all people. We leave the Good Friday services in silent awe, after venerating the cross and receiving the bread of our communion in that terrible and glorifying experience of Christ. Through Holy Saturday we stay in silence and fasting with the grief and expectant joy of this mystery as we wait to celebrate the Easter Vigil.

Assembling in the dark Holy Saturday night, we look to and follow the light of Christ symbolized in the new fire of the Easter candle and our own candles lit from that pillar. In Christ's light, praised in the *Exsultet*, we hear again in the images of Scripture the stories of salvation going on in us and our communities. We descend ritually into the waters of death in baptism and rise up in Christ's resurrected life. We eat and drink his transformed Body and Blood and are ourselves transformed in the joy of the Holy Spirit, singing the joyful Alleluia of this Easter Day dawning.

We rejoice in Easter feasting now for the fifty days that culminate in Pentecost, the full celebration of all Easter's gifts and fruits given in the Holy Spirit. As we continue on life's journey, we live in hope for the Easter of that Eternal Day in which our joy will never end.

April 9: Holy Thursday (Maundy Thursday)

Service Welcomed and Shared

Readings: Exod 12:1-8, 11-14; 1 Cor 11:23-26; John 13:1-15

Scripture:
Peter said to [Jesus], "You will never wash my feet."
Jesus answered him,
"Unless I wash you, you will have no inheritance with
me." (John 13:8)

Reflection: Once when I was visiting my family we were in the kitchen when we heard loud crying and wailing from our three- or four-year-old grandniece. My brother-in-law was "helping" her turn on the faucet at the sink in the bathroom. Later she confided her distress about that because, as she said, "I can do it myself!" Growing up we do need to learn and be allowed to do what we are able to do, and to keep developing our competence. But many of us grow up exaggerating the "I can do it myself" attitude. We have a rather pervasive and distorted notion that we are or can be in control of every situation in life. It is difficult for us to admit that there are times when we need help. We would prefer always to be the one helping. It can be difficult for us to be with others whom we are unable to help when they are physically, emotionally, or spiritually experiencing helplessness. That perhaps unconsciously undermines our self-image as the one who can always help, never needs to be helped.

Today Jesus is saying to Peter and to us, "You have to let yourself be helped and cared for. Before you can be anybody's helper, you need to be open to my help. Let your feet be washed. Receive the bread I am giving you, my self, my life. Drink the wine of my Blood that I am pouring out for you. Life, my life, is given for you. First receive it. Then you will be truly able to give it as my life and yours to others in service.

In word and sacrament today, we, with Peter and the other disciples, allow our feet to be washed by Christ; we receive and eat the bread of his Body; we drink the wine of his Blood. Together as one community we celebrate and deepen our need for and receptivity to his Loving Spirit and, in that Love, go out willing to receive from and humbly serve others.

Meditation: Consider ways you can graciously receive help from another. Watch for ways you can reach out graciously to help another.

Prayer: Wash our feet, Jesus, and show us how to wash those of others. Be the bread and wine that feeds our hunger for life, and show us how to share bread and life with others. We pray in gratitude for your love and example. Amen.

Transforming Love

Readings: Isa 52:13–53:12; Heb 4:14-16; 5:7-9; John 18:1–19:42

Scripture:
It was preparation day for Passover, and it was about
    noon.
And [Pilate] said to the Jews,
  "Behold, your king!"
They cried out,
  "Take him away, take him away! Crucify him!"
    (John 19:14-15a)

Reflection: The passion narrative of John is infinitely rich with shocking contrasts. From a garden of agony to a garden of peace. In the garden of agony, the great I AM. In the garden of peace, a dead human being. At the beginning, abandoned by friends; at the end, buried by acquaintances. An innocent charged and condemned as a criminal by a treacherous crowd and a spineless judge. Throughout the Passion a mocked, scourged, bruised and battered, crucified, unbelievable, ironic king with power over nothing, but claiming all is done by "power from above" (John). God in Jesus suffers the deepest degradation and pain of humanity. Our immediate response to John's Passion is profound silence at such suffering, such mystery, such deep tranquility radiating through it all. "Who would believe what we have heard?" (Isa 53:1a).

Jesus, in his deepest humiliation, betrayed, abandoned, denied, scourged, crowned with thorns and mocked, unjustly condemned, brutally nailed to a cross, manifests God as the king of another world, king in another dimension. Jesus, the bloodied and battered king, accepts and asserts his other-worldly dignity sometimes in silence and sometimes in sparse words cutting to the quick. He does not use power to dominate anyone, but rather to identify with every human being even, and especially, in her or his greatest suffering.

In Jesus we see Infinite Love longing for union with us not just in the good times, but also in the most wretched experiences of life—in our own suffering and in our inflicting suffering on others. The work Jesus has finished on the cross is the work of accepting us just as we are, staying with us even to the point of absorbing our cowardice, our violence, our hatred and hostility, so that in the caldron of divine Love we may be transformed.

Meditation: Before or after participating in the Good Friday service, find a quiet place, open to the presence of Christ with and in you and slowly read today's gospel aloud.

Prayer: Jesus, you have made the unbelievable infinite, unconditional love of God for us believable. Through our experience of this year's reading of your passion and death, bring us to deeper trust in that love so that we may extend it to others. Amen.

Dawn of a New Day

Readings: Gen 1:1–2:2 or 1:1, 26-31a; Gen 22:1-18 or 22:1-2, 9a, 10-13, 15-18; Exod 14:15–15:1; Isa 54:5-14; Isa 55:1-11; Bar 3:9-15, 32–4:4; Ezek 36:16-17a, 18-28; Rom 6:3-11; Mark 16:1-7

Scripture:
Since on the seventh day God was finished
  with the work he had been doing,
  he rested on the seventh day from all the work he had
    undertaken. (Gen 2:2)

Reflection: Tonight we listen to the Old Testament stories of God's work: creating for six full days; working with Abraham to bring him to a deeper faith; leading the Israelites forty years in the desert; sweeping the sea aside for them to pass through to freedom; calling back the faithless Israelites from exile and making plans for a new covenant and a new city bedecked with jewels; providing water, grain, wine, milk for the people at no cost, trying to get them to understand the divine ways and the effectiveness of God's word; pleading with the Israelites to listen and learn from the One "before whom the stars at their posts / shine and rejoice," answering when called, "'Here we are!' shining with joy for their Maker" (Bar 3:34-35); scattering the faithless and gathering them again, promising to give them a new heart and a new spirit. God's work done over weeks, decades, years, and eons is present here and now for us to enter into.

This is the night we have been waiting for. Tonight is the night, as we hear in the *Exsultet*, when God brings this divine work to completion, "breaking the chains of death, dispelling all evil, casting out hatred, bringing peace, reconciling all with God, bringing us into the light of the eternal day." All God's work comes to fruition in Jesus' life and death as the Spirit of God bursts through transforming Jesus into the risen Christ. Tonight this work of God in Christ is here for us to plunge into as we descend into and rise up from the baptismal waters, receive the anointing of his Holy Spirit, and eat the eucharistic meal together, rejoicing in his presence.

A new day is beginning to dawn. As the first light shimmers in the east, the sun begins its course through the everlasting day of the new creation. The world and all of its inhabitants have been transformed in the risen Christ. "Rejoice! Sing! Exult! Sound the trumpet!" Today's Morning Star, Christ, will never set.

Meditation: Do as little as possible today. Rest, prepare by slowly reading some of the Vigil Scripture passages, so that you can enter into God's work with an open ear and ready heart.

Prayer: Amazing God, your marvelous deeds evoke our unending praise. Accomplish your work in us, freeing us from sin and death, so that we may be your praise forever in Christ. Amen.

April 12: Easter Sunday

Christ Our Light

Readings: Acts 10:34, 37-43; Col 3:1-4 or 1 Cor 5:6b-8; John 20:1-9 or Mark 16:1-7 or, at an afternoon or evening Mass, Luke 24:13-35

Scripture:
On the first day of the week,
  Mary of Magdala came to the tomb early in the
    morning,
  while it was still dark,
  and saw the stone removed from the tomb. (John 20:1)

Reflection: Can you believe it? Easter is here! The tomb is empty! Christ is risen! Easter begins its flowering. That Morning Star that will never set sparkles joyfully through the early light of dawn. The Sun of our Eternal Day quietly emerges over the horizon. Jesus is risen and with us! Death and sin no longer have dominion!

Christ is risen: the Everlasting Morning of our Lenten nights of longing, the Loving Heart of all our prayer, the Eternal Feast of our fasting bodies/souls, the Riches of all our giving. Easter, the Day of our days, our Dancing Day, the day we celebrate Life conquering death, goodness conquering evil, is the source of lasting life, the fulfillment of all our hopes for never-failing love, for peace among all, for boundless happiness. Christ's victory of love transforms all our failures.

You may be at the tomb early this morning with Mary Magdalene while it is still dark, not seeing or feeling the Light of this new Day yet. Or maybe you are coming just as the sun rises. Whether in darkness or early morning Light, let yourself be amazed with her. Jesus' body is not here, only a young man clothed in white, saying, "Do not be amazed! You seek Jesus of Nazareth, the crucified. He has been raised; he is not here" (Mark 16:6). Jesus is not in the tomb; risen, he has ascended into a new dimension of life from which he, the cosmic Christ, the Lover of souls, is pouring out his Spirit into our body/spirits so that where he is we may follow. We are his body; his Spirit breathes in our spirits. On our journey through life and death, we travel with confidence and joyful love because Christ our Light, our Life, our Love, is drawing us with him into that new and everlasting dimension of life. Christ our Eternal Day.

Meditation: Wash, anoint yourself with oil, feast on the Bread of Life, drink the New Wine; remember and rejoice; shout and sing Amen, Alleluia! Christ is risen and with us!

Prayer: Risen Christ, you are the Dawn of a new day. You give us life through the waters of creation and baptism. Fill us with joyful hope and sustain us with the bread and wine of your Body and Blood through the power of your Spirit, so that together we can boldly proclaim this new Day not only in word but in loving action. Amen.

References

de Caussade, Jean-Pierre. *The Sacrament of the Present Moment*. San Francisco: Harper & Row, 1966, pp. 2, 4.

Downey, Michael. "Compassion." In *The New Dictionary of Catholic Spirituality*. Collegeville, MN: Liturgical Press, 1993, pp. 192–93.

RB 1980: The Rule of St. Benedict in English, edited by Timothy Fry. Collegeville, MN: Liturgical Press, 1981.

Greenleaf, Robert K. *Servant Leadership*. New York: Paulist Press, 1977.

Kennan, George. U.S. State Department Policy Planning, Study #23, February 24, 1948.

Levertov, Denise. *Sands of the Well*. New York: A New Directions Book, 1996, p. 123.

May, Gerald. *Will and Spirit: A Contemplative Psychology*. San Francisco: Harper & Row, 1982, pp. 5–6.

McDonnell, Kilian. "In the Kitchen." In *Swift, Lord, You Are Not*. St. John's University Press: Collegeville, MN, 2003, pp. 46–47.

Oliver, Mary. *Thirst*. Boston: Beacon Press, 2006.

Péguy, Charles. *God Speaks: Religious Poetry*, translated by Julian Green. New York: Pantheon Books, 1943, 1945, pp. 93–95.

The New Interpreter's Study Bible, edited by Katharine Doob Sakenfeld. Nashville, TN: Abingdon Press, 2003, p. 1783.

Schneiders, Sandra M. *Written That You May Believe: Encountering Jesus in the Fourth Gospel*. New York: Crossroad, 1999, pp. 79–80.

Selected Poetry of Jessica Powers, edited by Regina Siegfried and Robert Morneau. Kansas City, MO: Sheed & Ward, 1989.

Stuhlmueller, Carroll. *Biblical Meditations for Lent*. New York: Paulist Press, 1978, p. 59.